Pushing
The Pillars

Pushing
The Pillars

Karen Dunham

TATE PUBLISHING
AND ENTERPRISES, LLC

Published by Tate Publishing & Enterprises, LLC
127 E. Trade Center Terrace | Mustang, Oklahoma 73064 USA
1.888.361.9473 | www.tatepublishing.com

Tate Publishing is committed to excellence in the publishing industry. The company reflects the philosophy established by the founders, based on Psalm 68:11,
"The Lord gave the word and great was the company of those who published it."

Book design copyright © 2015 by Tate Publishing, LLC. All rights reserved.
Cover design by Carlo Nino Suico
Interior design by Jomar Ouano
Editors Lee Uzziah and Gayla Goodman

Published in the United States of America

ISBN: 978-1-63185-996-0
Biography & Autobiography / Religious
15.01.08

With all my heart I want to give a special thanks to the Lord who greatly encouraged me to move forward, to the Spirit who gave me the power, and to the Father who loved me all the way to the finish line.

This book is dedicated to Peter Blake Davis, my son who hears amazingly from God; Michael Hilsden, whose friendship stood the test of time; Robert and Virginia Dunham, who are the best parents in the world; and Stephen Harris who joins us in the race from heavenly places.

Acknowledgments

It is an honor to give a special acknowledgment to every volunteer who served or volunteered at Living Bread International Church in the promised land. To those who prayed for us, supported the move of his spirit with funding, and to them who sent their children to help us.

We also wish to acknowledge these inspiring brethren: Kim and Colton Mchone, Grace and Shawn Borgeson, Lila Hunt, Mark Plaisted, Richard Sherrod, Thomas Franks, Isaac Nuseibeh, Jakleen Hallaq, Noubar Vosgeritchian, Ceila Klaver, Hwei Fen, Florence Teo, Rev. John Dunham, Jody Dulmes, Deborah Gibbons, Lisa Hutcheson, Madeline Smith, Ron and Deborah Harris, Jeaniece Peppers, Michael Hilsden, Barry and Debra Davidson, Christy Thames, Tiffany and Daniel Lee, Connie and Bill Wilson, Suanne Barlow, Pastor Daphne and Yang Tuck Yoong, Victoria Bolton, Elvira Wawey, Apostle Paul, Samson, Karen and Ron Goodman.

Thank you to this editing team: Victoria Bolton, Jennifer Jefroimski, Deborah Harris, Karen Goodman, Lila Hunt, Ester Siu, Elizabeth Ryall, and Queen Adams.

Lord, please release special blessings and courage to the generation rising up, that it may be fearless and perfected in your love. Peter Blake Davis, Mike Hilsden, Sierra Schaefer, Cole Borgeson, Joseph Borgeson, Blake Borgeson. Thank You.

Thank you Rotem, Idan, Daniel, and the other liaison officers who encouraged us to keep running the race.

Thank you Deborah Harris and Jeaniece Peppers, whom God uses to keep the army of God praying for us while we fight the good fight.

Contents

Grinder in the Prison

"Death of Samson" by Gustave Dore

I woke up, as I often did, after sleeping off a heavy dose of drinking. I was still in bed when I opened my eyes and noticed bars on my windows. I thought to myself, *I must be dreaming*. So I closed my eyes again and drifted back to sleep. After sleeping a little longer,

I slowly began to awaken. This time, I thought to myself, *Oh no, this is for real.* Reality started to set in. I was in prison. I began thinking back and wondered, *How did I get in this place?* I flashed back. Oh, yeah. I had been working as a waitress at a restaurant called The Judge's Chambers. It happened to be located across the street from the Pinellas County courthouse. One day, an ex-con came into the restaurant. He asked if anyone wanted to buy some quaaludes. A person had to buy a minimum of two hundred. I did not really know anyone who would want that many, but the guy said he would give me the pills to sell, and I could pay him later.

As soon as I stepped outside the door of the restaurant, two policemen cocked their guns and pointed them to my head and then arrested me. The narcotics officers wanted me to find men in bars interested in buying drugs or pot. Their idea was to use me as a snitch prostitute for them. Their plan would be to go to their houses afterward and bust them for drugs. I had led a pretty rough life—far over the edge. But this was something I was not willing to do, and I refused to cooperate with them. When we made our court appearance, the officers testified against me and said that I was uncooperative. The ruling was a harsh one, and the judge gave me the maximum sentence.

Before I went to prison, I would wake up some mornings with no idea where my car was. I often had to wander around on Sunday afternoons in search of my car. Many times, I woke up in strange houses with men I had never seen before.

I never acknowledged or knew the Lord, but I had met enough demons in my life to know that the devil was real. I used to get angry when people would pray around me. My younger brother was a solemn Baptist, and sometimes, when our family was all together, sharing a meal, he would say a prayer. This really angered and upset me. I wanted no praying around me.

Flashbacks in prison to my younger years led me to reflect upon some of my experiences. I lay there thinking, *Prison—just another stop on the highway to hell.*

Looking back today, I am reminded of Samson, who was blinded when both his eyes were pierced out of his head. The enemy would mock him while he performed as a grinder in the prison. Today, I know that I was used by the devil to do a lot of things as a prisoner of sin.

> Then the Philistines took him and put out his eyes, and brought him down to Gaza. They bound him with bronze fetters, and he became a grinder in the prison.

> Judges 16:21 (NKJV)

As I reflected back to my teenage years, I recalled jumping out of my bedroom window and sneaking off to all-night parties. I was regularly drunk out of my mind. I was only seven or eight years old when one of my male babysitters and his friends molested me. When my dad came home that night, I told him what had happened. Those men never returned after my father finished scolding them. At different times in my childhood, my parents would stick me in foster homes with strangers for misbehaving. People at school used to ask if I had parents, and when I told them that I did, they would wonder why I was put in foster care. I never had a good answer for them, but I had a habit of attracting a lot of adversity because of my rebellious lifestyle. My life was pitiful. Those foster homes had some real problems. Some of those people were drinkers and had their own problems with perversion.

While living in my own home at age eleven, a neighbor peeked in the window to watch me bathe. My dad went out and beat the man up. The same thing happened later in foster care, but it was a foster dad who I caught peeking at me while I bathed then. The world seemed really messed up to me back then, and I had no dreams of doing or being anything in my life. I felt inferior and utterly alone.

Staring up at the bars in prison, I realized how sick my life was and what a dead end I had come to. My first thirty days in prison were spent in R & O (Reception and Orientation), which was a type of evaluation. They would give us a liquid tranquilizer every day. There were women inside cutting each other with knives, and many of them were in lesbian relationships. I think some of them entered those relationships out of fear.

At the end of thirty days, they moved me to another location within the prison called Forest Hills. Since it was designated for low-risk prisoners, there were no security bars. My roommate, Thelma, was serving a sentence for having murdered her husband. She said he had beaten her over and over so many times that she finally killed him.

While in Forest Hills, I read every single book on the prison cart except the Bible. When I finished reading all the books, there was just that one book sitting there on the cart left to read. That was the one book I had no interest in reading at that point in my life.

I remember watching two lesbians as they made their way back and forth to the prison church. They were busy planning their wedding, anticipating their release so they could be married. Witnessing those two made me think the church was just as sick as the rest of the world.

I thought about my father while I was in prison. When I was a little girl, he would beat me so badly that you could barely see the skin on parts of my body. My grandmother had worried that he might end up killing me.

Sometime back in the seventies, I walked into the social affairs office. It was a brand-new division, and many of the employees had long hair and looked like hippies. I met a man that was going to give me some help, but I thought, if this long-haired dude shows up at my father's house, I will either be beaten to death or end up in some foster home forever.

I was nothing short of amazed when the social worker finally did go speak with my father. I did not know it then, but I know today that God was with me. God was with me even when I did not know he was there. I never heard a word of what was spoken between the social worker and my father, but I was never beaten again. My father stopped drinking too. I was and am very proud of my father.

Despite our difficult past, my father was good to me while I was doing time in prison. My mother, on the other hand, did not write to me, and she refused to discuss me with others because she was so ashamed. But my father was faithful. He would regularly wire me eighty dollars, which was the maximum amount of money we were allowed to receive in the prison at that time. My father was the only friend I had while in prison. I knew he did not have any money to give, but he was steadfast in sending it to me. This was the mercy of God, whom I did not know. I loved my earthly father very much for helping me, and I understood my mother. I had a lot of shame on myself.

Released from Prison

Peter Blake Davis

Being released from prison felt like a bad dream had finally ended. I vowed never to return. I began selling fleets of used cars, bought houses, and acquired money. I managed to stay away from illegal drugs, but on the inside, my spiritual life had not changed any, and my heart was full of corruption. I felt very inferior and was extremely afraid of people in authority. During those years, I had many abortions and several drunken and drugged up nights. I had stopped selling drugs but had not stopped using them. Instead of using illegal drugs, I would obtain them legally by prescription from local doctors.

At one point, I ended up pregnant with twins and was distraught when I lost them. I became very upset with God and asked him why he took them. It was the first time I actually had a conversation with God, so I guess I knew he was there. I also knew I was full of sin. I was complaining to him about his judgment in taking my babies, yet I had never acknowledged him before this. Upon the death of my twins, I knew God had the power over life and death.

In 1986, I was involved with a married man and became pregnant again. When I told him I was expecting, he let me know that he was not interested in raising another family. I told him that was okay, but I was going to keep the baby. I loved my son Peter, also known as Blake, so much. People around me remarked that they had never seen such a relationship as I had with my son. As a young boy, my son, Blake, looked like an angel and would laugh all the time. I was so happy just looking at Blake and being with him. I promised myself I would never beat him like my brothers and I were beaten as kids.

I did not raise my son to know Jesus Christ, but I enrolled him in the Christian preschool at Trinity Church, and I hired an ex-nun to be his babysitter. I felt I could trust those people, even though I personally did not put my trust in God, nor did I know him.

Mafia Terror

Twenty years after being released from prison, I was living in Safety Harbor, a little town in central Florida. At that time, I had acquired my real estate license, and I had bought and sold nearly fifty homes. I had also sold masses of automobiles, and I personally owned multiple vehicles, a boat, a motor home, a gas station, and several houses.

I did not receive a high level of education. I said to myself, "I have a lot of money, and I can buy anything I want, yet one day I will go straight to hell." I thought maybe that just before I died, I would get right with God, but then again I thought, *Who needs God?*

My brother was a diagnosed schizophrenic. He did not make a lot of money like I did, so I wanted to help him out. I bought a property with two houses on it. I divided the property and sold the front portion of it to get my money back and gave the remaining house to my brother as a gift.

Later, a lawyer from Tampa Bay courthouse sold the house I had given my brother at a sheriff's sale in a case of stolen identity. I was livid. How could this lawyer get away with this? A passion for justice burned inside of me to obtain justice for my brother. I went to the courthouse and began an investigation into the lawyer's activities. I had wisdom I never knew before and thought to myself, *Where did all this understanding come from?*

I found out the attorney had manipulated case files. He had falsified the order from the judge and was manipulating the court docket. I filed a complaint with the Florida bar association, the governor's office, the Secret Service, and the Federal Bureau of Investigation. I could look at files in the courthouse records, and I could tell when the microfiche was missing. It was like I had the lights turned on in my head as I worked toward building the case. I learned so much about the corruption in probate. I learned about the stealing of people's identities, properties, and inheritances as I worked on preparing my case against the lawyer.

In the end, I uncovered information that was very sensitive and ended up with the Mafia after me. It was not the Mafia found in strip joints; these guys worked in business suits and as lawyers.

One might ask, "How did you know the Mafia was after you?" Well, it became clear one day after I made a service call to my phone company. A technician came and opened the box at my house. When I took a look at what he showed me, I almost fainted. There were twenty-seven phone lines running through my house. There should have only been two! The repairman asked, "Why are there twenty-seven lines in here?" That's when I knew for certain I was in serious trouble. I felt a deep dread come over me. I walked into the house and took a good look at the ceiling. The tongue and groove pine was riddled with small holes and with wires that went from the telephone box to hidden surveillance cameras. I cut the lines and tried to pull them out of the phone box, but there were more lines underneath the house.

My life soon became a big nightmare. One night, I was sitting on the couch with my son, and I saw black powder seeping into the room from the vents. We were being gassed! I covered my son in a blanket as he lay sleeping on the couch. I pressed my face against the window screen and saw a large man standing outside our door. I knew that if we tried to go outside, this man would hurt us, so I shut off all the electricity in the house and kept going to the windows to get a breath of fresh air. My son seemed to be in a very deep sleep. I had to drag the couch with him lying on it over to the window so he could breathe. I kept my eye on the shadow of the man as I watched through the window. My teeth were rattling with fear.

My Christian brother had given me a couple of pistols. I wanted to shoot through the door at that man standing on the other side, waiting for me to come out. I knew no matter what I said, I would end up back in prison if I were to fire one shot. Still, I walked around with loaded guns in my pockets. I slept with them, and when I went to the store, I kept them hidden in my car.

During that time, we suffered several attacks by those people. They tried to intimidate us on the phone by placing strange objects in our house and by sending men to stand around outside our door. I thought they were trying to drive me into a mental hospital. The food in the refrigerator looked like a chemical garden; the eggs had a green glow to them. I knew my son and I were being poisoned and drugged. Both of us looked like we had eaten rat poison for a long period of time. We were grayish in color, and I knew time was running out.

Every time I called 911 or any other emergency number, a man would pick up and say, "If you quit, we will quit." They were obviously spending thousands of dollars in trying to keep me quiet, but I was not about to stay quiet. I went to agency after agency, trying to find help and some kind of justice for the lawyer who had stolen my brother's property.

I was assigned two FBI agents in Tampa, Florida. I met them once, and when I returned to their office, both agents were gone. The woman at the desk said they were called out on other jobs. No one seemed to know what was going on. I talked to a reporter, and not long after, she too could not be reached. Some Secret Service agents promised to help me as well, but no matter whom I talked to, the people always disappeared. We just could not get any real help. We were in very serious trouble, and we were getting nowhere. From our research into the courthouse corruption, I knew those people were stealing a lot of money and property out of probate. I also knew that at least one man had been killed to cover it up. I thought, *They must think I know much more than what I really know.*

One day, I called the police because we were being terrorized yet again. My niece Mary and I found a really heavy clock inside our house, and we were afraid there was a bomb inside of it. This time, two men appeared at my door dressed in police uniforms, with guns and a squad car. They had runny noses and looked like they had been doing drugs for quite a while. They came into my house, and one of the men told me to go get my son, who was asleep at the end of the hall. One of the guys put on a pair of rubber gloves and ordered, "Go get your son," as he touched the gun at his side. As I began walking down the hallway to wake up my son, I thought to myself, *I must be out of my mind. There is no way those men are real police officers.* The way the men kept sniffling and wiping their noses, I was sure they were high on cocaine. They acted strangely, and they looked as scared as I was. I returned to the living room and told the men my son was sleeping, so I was not going to get him up. My niece was sitting on the couch, looking terrified, so I said to the men, "Let's go outside and talk." Once I was outside talking to them, I told them I needed to go back and check on something. As I went in, I quickly closed the door behind me and locked it. They drove off immediately.

They terrorized me in my house for about six months. I was very afraid for my son, Blake. At that time, he walked to the school at the end of the block every day, and I was worried sick they would take him or hurt him. Thugs walked in front of the school or sat on the street side just to intimidate us. My hair treatment had been tampered with, which caused my hair to fall out. It had been like washing my head with acid. Once, when cleaning the house, I saw what looked like a real eyeball just lying there on the floor. Eventually, I looked behind the refrigerator and found a package about six inches long. I took it to my aunt who owned a radio and television shop, and she told me it was a military resistor. I was certain the entire house had a lot of radiation running through it. Another day, I went to get the mail, and a live centipede was in an envelope in our personal mailbox. Fear was what the Mafia operated in, and I had it running through my body. My teeth rattled, and I had adrenaline rushes flowing through me from fear. It seemed like the evil onslaught coming at us would never end.

My Friend Chris

Chris, who was one of my best friends, knew the trouble I was having, and she invited me to come stay at her house for the weekend. She definitely had problems of her own. Her boyfriend would beat her when he was drunk. Chris said she felt bad hearing about all the things we were going through. She wanted to spend time with me and comfort me, but while I was there, really strange things happened. It was as if I had entered another bad dream. I had taken a few pictures for evidence against the Mafia with my camera. When I arrived at her home, I placed my camera on her counter top, but a couple of hours later, my camera went missing.

Then, her boyfriend George talked me into taking my Jeep over to a station to get it cleaned and checked out. I had been under attack by the Mafia for about six months, and I was apprehensive at the prospect of letting the Jeep out of my sight, but George was very insistent. I handed it over to him with dread in my heart. He promised to loan me the car outside if I needed to go anywhere. The next day, I did borrow it to go visit a friend. When I got to my friend's house and opened up the trunk of the car, I discovered it was loaded with drugs. They looked like quaaludes, with needles, syringes, and other drugs. I knew by my previous time in prison that the trunk contained enough drugs to have me put away for life.

I could not believe what was happening. I entered a state of shock. My teeth were rattling, and I was shuddering uncontrollably by the time I entered my friend Steve's house. Before I became a realtor, he had taught me how to buy and sell houses. I carried the drugs and needles inside his house, put them into a trash bag, and then hurled them into his garbage can. I knew in my heart if I had tried to tell the authorities what happened, I would have been arrested.

Later, back at Chris's house, I found myself staring at a large houseplant next to where I was sitting. It looked strange to me, so I went over and tried to move it. It was too heavy to move. When I asked her about it, she seemed scared. She gave me the quiet sign with her finger over her lips. Her house was obviously bugged, and she knew it.

Later that night, when her boyfriend came home, he gave me some Coca-Cola to drink. I had some of it. That night, while I was lying in bed, I saw a little metal object falling out of the vent. At that point, I was so out of it that I knew my Coca-Cola had been drugged and that I was being gassed again. I felt my lungs ripping apart as I continuously coughed in the cloudy room. Chris and George came into the room, and they were looking all around for the metal capsule that had ignited with gas. I pointed over to where the capsule was. I knew they thought I was so drugged that I would never remember all this.

The next night, at bedtime, George gave me another drink. When they were not looking, I poured it all out. As soon as I got in my bedroom that night, I shut the vent before going to bed. I heard George talking on the phone with someone (I presumed it was the Mafia), saying that everything was going according to plan. Later that night, I heard the noise of the metal capsule hitting the back of the vent I had closed. That night, they could not touch me, and I knew it was time to move on.

The next day, I came out of my room and demanded they give me my Jeep back. I wanted to get out of there as soon as I could. I realized that my friend had sold me out to the Mafia because she was desperate to get her son, who had been busted out of prison. Later on, she told me she had been infected with some kind of strange disease, so she felt she had to cooperate with them. Chris kept putting her hand to her lips and telling me to be quiet. At that point, it seemed like I was in a bad dream; a horror movie and I could not get out. I felt I was dangling over the pits of hell and the only thing preventing me from falling in were the hands that were holding onto me by my feet. I know today that it was Jesus Christ who had my feet, or they would have killed me many times. I did not know him, but he loses none the Father has given him, and I belonged to him.

Meeting Jesus Christ

One day, my sister-in-law, who was a Southern Baptist missionary, said, "Why don't you come and spend the night with us? I think it will do you some good to get out of the house." It sounded like a good idea. I knew my days were numbered. With men being posted outside and us being drugged, gassed, and terrorized, I felt like someone was going to die. I responded with a yes, as I felt this deep dread in me. I knew that the end was near.

Blake was only nine years old at that time, and I was forty. We packed a little suitcase and went over to her house. We were at her home, inside her living room, when she took a good look at me and asked me, "Do you want Jesus to help you?" I thought about it and realized Jesus was the only one I had not asked for help. I said, "Yes, I do want Jesus to help us."

Wendy said, "To get Jesus to help you, you have to get down on your knees." Blake and I got on our knees. We both repeated what she said, "Jesus, come into our hearts." All of a sudden, it was like a blanket of peace coming over us. Nothing mattered anymore. I was no longer afraid of the Mafia because Jesus Christ had given us peace. All fear was gone. My teeth stopped rattling, and the adrenaline rushes ceased. The terror had disappeared.

She asked me if I wanted to get baptized. My son and I both answered yes. Wendy handed me a book called *The Promises of God*. We stayed the night and decidedly felt a change come over us. We were in a place of peace that neither one of us had ever known before.

While I was in the spare bedroom that night, something weird happened. Some kind of electrical current struck me and stayed on me. It was very painful, and I felt like I was being electrocuted. I was thinking, *Could this house be wired too, or is the anti-Christ after me now?* I was down on the floor, racked with darts of pain shooting through me. But no matter how much pain I suffered, no matter how much terror we endured, we now had Jesus Christ with us. The peace and comfort of that knowledge was beyond words and greater than the pain. We were not alone in our battle any longer, and we knew he had us in the palm of his hand.

Involuntary Sheriff Order

When we returned to our house, I started reading the book called *The Promises of God* to Blake. I read scriptures that said the Lord would heal our diseases. I had taken a lot of prescription drugs, and Blake was on Ritalin. Blake never seemed right after taking the Ritalin, so I used to take most of it myself. According to what I read, Jesus Christ was saying that I did not need those drugs, and neither did Blake. We were so happy with all the promises. I went into Blake's room and said, "You do not need this Ritalin anymore." We threw it all out. We threw out every drug in the house. Blake loved hearing me read the scriptures about 'fear not' before falling to sleep.

> Praise the LORD, my soul, and forget not all his benefits—
> who forgives all your sins and heals all your diseases,
>
> Psalm 103:2–3 (NIV)

> But now thus saith the LORD that created thee, O Jacob, and
> he that formed thee, O Israel, Fear not: for I have redeemed
> thee, I have called thee by thy name; thou art mine.
>
> Isaiah 43:1 (KJV)

I knew in the spirit that Satan had just been dealt a big blow. No longer did we see men posted at our door. Everything in our lives had changed since we had Jesus Christ to lean on. I really felt the Mafia was afraid of Christ. I bought cassette recordings of the Bible from a local Christian bookstore and began playing the tapes as often as I possibly could. I listened to my Bible tapes all hours of the day and night.

It was not much later that I went to my parents and told them I was a Christian. However, they thought I had some serious mental issues. They kept saying, "We want the old Karen back." I told them I was following and serving Jesus Christ. When they heard this, they thought there must be something seriously wrong with me.

I was talked into making an appointment with a child psychiatrist in Tampa, whom I had sold a medical building to. During the appointment, I told the doctor that my son no longer needed to take Ritalin or any other drugs. I proceeded to tell him that we had Jesus Christ now and that he was going to heal us of everything.

After the appointment, the doctor called my father and advised him that they should have me committed immediately because he said that when people start talking about Jesus Christ, it was the end of the rope. It was time to have me committed. The doctor told my father that he needed to get my son away from me as soon as possible because he thought I might hurt him. My father went and picked up the involuntary medical order from the sheriff, which had been signed by the doctor, to commit me to a mental institution.

Before he did anything with the sheriff's order, my father came to me and, with sadness in his eyes, said, "I have already lost one son to a mental institution, and I do not want to lose another child."

I said to him, "I forgive you, Dad. I am not crazy. Jesus Christ is really helping me."

Crying, he gave me the involuntary medical order signed by the doctor. I still have it, as a reminder of that day. I thank Jesus Christ who saved me from the lion's den of the mental institution. I knew in my heart I would have been killed by the Mafia had they been successful in committing me.

# Leaving It All Behind

My family still wanted the old Karen back. By the grace of God, my father did not have me committed to a mental institution. The Mafia was still after me, but the most important thing was that I now had Jesus Christ. It was such an incredible and wonderful feeling in my heart. Jesus Christ was with me and would never leave.

One day, I told Blake that I felt God wanted us to leave Clearwater, Florida. I believed God was telling us that we needed to sell everything. I felt he wanted us to have an estate sale and leave the area. At the sale, someone asked me, "Who died?"

I said, "No one."

In my heart, I knew it was a sweet victory to have an estate sale and yet to be alive. I could not wait to get to the church and give them money. It was thrilling to be able to sow unto the King who had rescued me.

After the massive sale, including the sale of our house, all we had left was the Jeep and a motor home. We took the motor home on the road to a Christian campground in Flat Rock, North Carolina, that we had found in the yellow pages.

That was to be our new home, but the Mafia followed us there as well.

Power in the Word

Once in the Christian campground, I met Daphne and her husband. They were on a lot of prescription medicines. Daphne told me the United States government had used her father's farmland for various experiments. Daphne's father and one of her brothers died because of a chemical they had been experimenting with. She also told me that when she served in the army, she had been raped inside a cooler. Daphne was manifesting all kinds of paranoia and schizophrenia and needed major deliverance.

At that time, I had known the Lord for only about a year and a half, so I was still a young Christian. I kept thinking that if Daphne would ask Jesus Christ into her heart, he would deliver her. I knew in my spirit that she did not have a personal relationship with Jesus Christ, so I told her, "You have to get Jesus in your heart." Daphne said she was already a Catholic Christian. I told her, "No, you have to invite him inside your heart." We prayed for the blood of Jesus Christ to wash away her sins and for the Lord to give her deliverance. We both enjoyed the peace that came over her. I was so impressed with the Lord, with the fact that we could pray and see change right before our eyes.

Later, at another meeting with Daphne, I felt the Lord was telling me to pray for the armor of God to come upon her. We were in the small living room of our motor home when I put my hand on her shoulder and started praying,

Stand therefore, having girded your waist with truth, having put on the breastplate of righteousness,

Ephesians 6:14 (NKJV)

When I got to the part about the breastplate, Daphne fell to the floor. She looked at me and said, "Man, this armor is some pretty heavy stuff!" I took a look at my Bible and thought to myself, *There is a lot more power in speaking his word than meets the eye.* I told her I thought God wanted her to rest. I sat down and was in awe of the power of God. I wanted to see what else I could find on power in the Bible. My heart was on a journey of discovery. I was so intrigued with God!

God Comes Through Again

One day, as I drove up to our motor home, I caught a glimpse of a man inside. Blake was in the car with me. God had told me to stop speaking to him about the Mafia because it was hurting him and scaring him too much, so I just kept driving and returned to our home later. I knew the man was inside our home and trying to poison us, so we praised the Lord. No matter what they tried to do to us, it did not affect us. On several occasions, they turned our gas on and disconnected it from the stove, causing gas to pour into our house. They did many things to try and terrorize us.

The Lord connected me with a group of wonderful women from many denominations who had been praying together for more than thirty years. They took me under their wings. There was a different prayer meeting at the campground, where a pastor had told me that I did not have the Holy Spirit because I didn't pray in tongues. I was sure I had him though, since he was such a great comfort to me. I loved God with everything within me. He had rescued me from the serpent, and I was his forever.

Another time, I was praying on the phone with one of the spiritual mothers from Flat Rock. There was some oil sitting on the table, and I saw Blake put some on his finger and walk over to me. He put some of it on my forehead. I turned to him and asked, "What did you do that for?"

He said, "God told me to do it because he has called you to be his servant." With that, he turned and walked out the door and jumped on his skateboard. I am constantly amazed by the simplicity of God and of the gospel. I recounted this to my friend on the phone, and we were both rejoicing over what God had done.

One night, I was invited to a meeting where they were teaching about healing. While I was walking back home after the meeting, the front of my foot flipped under. The pain was excruciating. It felt as though my ankle was trying to come through the bridge of my foot. I was barely able to crawl into our motor home. Blake saw me and started crying, "Mom, I have to call an ambulance."

I said, "All right, honey. You can call the ambulance, but let's pray first."

I crawled over to a chair. Never had I felt pain like that before. Blake and I began to pray, and suddenly, there was a feeling of spinning, which started from the top of my toe. It continued up my foot and through my leg. This was a spin in the Spirit. I could feel the Lord healing me, and I said to Blake, "Keep praying for me. God is healing me." I could feel the spin getting faster and faster. By the time it ran all the way up my leg, I was completely healed.

That was a mighty manifestation of healing from the Lord. I witnessed his power, and at that point in my spiritual walk, I really felt like nothing was impossible for God. He was such a good Father, and I never loved anything or anyone as much as I loved God. He was everything to me, and I was so happy he had found me.

Moving Again

We were in Flat Rock for a while until one day when we thought God might be moving us. When Blake and I looked up to the clouds and saw the word *Atlanta* written on them, we knew it was time to go to Atlanta. God is the God of the impossible. He will communicate with you if your heart is open to hear. Blake and I looked at each other, rejoicing, and said, "Let's go to Atlanta!"

Back then, we had the word of God playing day and night. When I put Blake to bed, I would still read *The Promises of God* to him. We knew the Mafia was still following us, even with all the moving we had done. Jesus Christ was the only reason we were safe and alive. We clung to Jesus and his word as tightly as possible because we both knew that God had his protection on us and that nothing could take us off this earth unless God allowed it to happen.

On our way back to Atlanta, a black Mercedes Roadster passed us on the road, and the driver motioned us to pull off to the side. We knew he was trying to scare us, and when he passed us, we saw his license plate. It read "666." We continued driving the speed limit in our motor home. As we continued a bit further, we saw a flame of fire spread across the road. Praise God that the Lord had told me to close the open gas valve under our motor home before we left. He delivered us as we drove right through the fire. Through those terrible times, he delivered us again and again. The King was on the road with us now, and no weapon formed against us would prosper. It was wonderful to be in his care.

My Son Wants You for a Bride

Dancing on the walls of Jerusalem

Next, we ended up in a KOA campground in Atlanta. At that time, I started having radical encounters with God. One night, the Father appeared to me with Jesus next to him. The images were in a heavenly vision that I had not witnessed before. I saw silhouettes of two men's heads, and the Father said, "My Son wants you for a bride."

I said yes. That night, there was a radical encounter of love with the King. The next morning, I was still completely shaken. With that incredible encounter, I felt out of my natural senses. I kept reliving what had happened to me and how Jesus Christ wanted to take me as his bride. I bundled myself up in a blanket to hide, but Jesus was inside the bundle with me. An incredible amount of love was pouring out of him. I was saturated with his love. My whole body was dripping with his love, and I began to shake. It felt like lightning bolts from heaven shooting through my body.

Every day, he drenched me with his love, which drove away all my fear. His breath was on my face, and his arms were wrapped around me. I had visions of him and words from him. It was like being in heaven, but I was still here on earth. I woke up hearing his voice speaking blessings to me, and I felt rivers of blessings flowing through my body. Once my body had felt his astounding love, there was no way anyone was going to take it away from me. It was greater than drugs or fine wine. Experiencing his waterfalls of his love washing over me every morning was like living in paradise.

I was surrounded and immersed in the favor and anointing of God. While Blake was at school, I would spend all day just drowning in the love of Jesus. When he looked into my eyes, my body would manifest his love. Those pools of destiny would bore into me. I never wanted to leave the look of his gaze. To this day, his love controls me and will never let me go. I am driven by his love, his grace, and his mercy upon my life. To know the love of God is inexpressible. His love is available for the least all the way to the greatest on earth to experience.

> and though you have not seen him, you love him, and though you do not see him now, but believe in him, you greatly rejoice with joy inexpressible and full of glory,
>
> 1 Peter 1:8 (NASB)

One day, the Lord gave me an extremely wonderful encounter with him. I was sitting next to him in the heavens and looking at the world. His presence was incredibly strong as I sat in a very special place near him. I felt intensely favored to be there by his side, and I could feel his longing and love for his inheritance—the nations. I never wanted to move from that place seated next to the Lord.

> Before long, the world will not see me anymore, but you will see me.
>
> John 14:19a (NIV)

I believe that promise. Do not ever let anyone steal the blessing of knowing him and being known by him. You were created to be in fellowship with the Lord. In his presence and in his hands is an eternal blessing that will be with you when you meet him in glory. Do not stop drawing close to him. He is worth giving up everything for. You will never be sorry for saying yes to Jesus Christ.

After a year or so of spiritual encounters with the Lord, I knew that I was born again. The vision was so real to me that I could feel his touch. The best explanation I can give is that I was in a shell that was cracking open like a baby bird hatching out of an egg. The Lord washed me as I came out of the cracked shell, and as he held me up in his hand, he put me into a basket. I felt like I was the size of an ant in that little basket. The love and the smile radiating from the Father as he looked into my eyes could not be described or put into words. It was life-changing to see him smile and to feel his love. I had become a work of his hands.

> For you have been born again, not of perishable seed, but of imperishable, through the living and enduring word of God.
>
> 1 Peter 1:23 (NIV)

The Birth of Living Bread
International Church

A few years later, feeding the poor in Jericho

We lived in the KOA campground in Atlanta for about six months. While we were in the campground, Blake came into the house one day and said, "God told me to tell you to go to the grocery store, and they will give you bread. He said you are going to give bread to the poor."

When Blake heard from the Lord, I had learned to really listen to what he said. I called the Kroger grocery store and asked about day-old bread for the poor. The first thing he asked me was, "What is the name of your company?" Since I didn't have a name, I told the guy I would have to call him back. I was still trying to think of a good name when Blake came into the house and said, "God said we are to call our organization Living Bread." He added, "Mom, if you do not use this name, you will be in sin." That day, we became Living Bread.

The Kroger manager said he would like to give us everything they could no longer sell. The favor of God was so heavy upon us. It was amazing living in a little motor home and picking up loads of bread for the poor. I gave the bread and gospel tracts to those who were trying to kick alcohol and drugs. Those gospel tracts came from Mr. Peters in Clearwater, Florida. A few days a week, I would load up my little wagon with day-old bread and wait for God to tell me which direction to drive. He would lead me into poor neighborhoods, trailer parks, halfway houses, and at times, we would even stop on the side of the road.

I really believed God and was so thankful to be used in the ministry that he had given me. I knew God was pleased with me, and I became so grateful. All my life, I had never been chosen by men for anything, but now the Ruler of the Universe had me working for him. I felt so important to God and extremely loved.

At that time, I attended Northgate Church in Atlanta. Different prophets would visit our church, and one night, a speaker came and spoke of how they had handed out a lot of gospel tracts over the years. He said it had been a waste of time and money. When I heard that, I was shaken. That was my assignment from God. We gave bread to the poor and handed out gospel tracts. So I asked God to let me see some of the fruit of the work he had given me.

The next day, I picked up a load of bread and gospel tracts. I headed to a trailer park where I had been before. As I was driving through the park, the driver of a little white truck motioned me to stop. A girl jumped out of the truck, ran over to me, and was so excited she could hardly catch her breath. She began to tell me her story, "A few months ago you passed by while I was sitting on the porch with my boyfriend. You handed us a loaf of bread and a gospel tract. I read the gospel tract and then moved out of my boyfriend's house. Now I am living with my mother, and I live for the Lord." I was amazed at the goodness of the Lord. He was giving me great encouragement just when I needed it. I was hearing from God and doing what he wanted me to do. No matter what anyone said, it felt wonderful to be his chosen one, on a holy mission for him.

The people who lived in the KOA campground were very poor. One family was living in a camper that was so full of stuff that I wondered where the children slept. They were very thankful for the bread that we gave them.

One time, when a little neighbor girl named Brook and I were worshipping, I gave her one of our flags to wave. Now the flag was about as big as she was, and she started waving it frantically. I asked her, "Is it time to put the flag up?"

Brook was very confident in her answer, "No, Jesus said he just started his engines."

I loved how the Lord ministered and spoke through children. One day, a little girl named Summer kissed the Bible and started laughing. I asked her why she was laughing and she said, "When I kissed the Bible, Jesus kissed me back!"

God is a God of relationships. He will take you places and reveal himself to you. You must slow down and take the time to get to know him. It is the greatest thing on this earth you can do—to know the Lord and to give your heart to him.

> But without faith it is impossible to please him, for he who comes to God must believe that he is, and that he is a rewarder of those who diligently seek him.
>
> Hebrews 11:6 (NKJV)

Ronnie

Communion

Blake had a friend named Ronnie who came to spend the night with us. The two boys were going to the roller rink on the following day. Part of our agreement was that they would both go with me to a Messianic church. Before we left for church, I told Ronnie that Blake and I were going to do Communion. When I asked Ronnie if he knew Jesus, he said he did not, but he wanted to. Ronnie prayed and asked Jesus into his heart. I invited him to share Communion with us, and I started telling him about the flesh and the blood of Jesus. I told him all about what Jesus did on the cross, and I gave each of us a piece of bread and a small cup of grape juice. The next thing I knew, Ronnie was breaking off a big piece of the matza. He said, "If this is Jesus, I need a lot more of him."

Blake and I just grinned and went off to church. After church, the Sunday school teacher looked amused. Ronnie had told everyone in the class that he had Jesus in his heart and then proceeded to ask each of the kids, "Do you have Jesus in your heart?"

The next day, before I dropped them off at the skating rink, Ronnie said, "Can I have a Communion bread cracker and some blood?" So I gave him a little sleeve of cups, a bottle of grape juice and some matza. I said, "Here, you can do this when you get home." I dropped them off at the roller rink, but when I returned to pick them up, Ronnie's dad was standing at the doorway. He asked, "What happened to Ronnie? The first thing he said to me was, 'Do you have Jesus in your heart?'" I smiled and went in to get my son.

I found Blake, and he told me, "Mom, all day long, Ronnie was making the kids come and sit with him around the table so he could share Communion with them. Ronnie ran up to me and said, "All my friends did Communion with me, but my sister would not drink the blood."

Ronnie had a remarkable gift of evangelism.

Our New House

One day, out of the blue, Blake's father called and said, "I had a dream last night that I helped you buy a house." I said, "Yes, we really want to move out of the campground." We found a house in Alpharetta, Georgia, and bought it on a contract for deed. The owner agreed to hold the deed in escrow until we paid for the house. We used our last little bit of funds along with a gift from Blake's dad to make the down payment.

We were able to move into the house but had to rent out a room to help pay the mortgage. My tenant used to say that toys, movies, books, and games were all demonic. From the way she talked, it seemed that everything the kids were interested in was demonic. It influenced me to the point where I got carried away and did things I should not have done, like throwing out my son's new toys that he loved. That extreme strictness damaged my relationship with my son, but I only realized later that it was totally driven by a religious spirit. I have now learned, through many lessons with children, that you build them up from wherever they are at. God is an encourager, one who edifies his children.

The Mafia was still following us and continually doing nasty things to us, but we had long since learned to not talk to other people about what was happening. Blake and I pretended the Mafia did not exist. When we moved into our new house, I ordered a stove. It was wintertime and very cold. The house had a gas fireplace, but the lighter kept going out when I tried to light it. One of the repairmen went into the kitchen and found that the gas pipe had been disconnected from the stove. The gas was turned on full blast and coming out of the wall, so he opened all the windows to let it out. He was absolutely livid at the gas company because he thought they had made the mistake when they hooked up my new stove.

I knew in my heart it was the Mafia trying to take us out again. When the Mafia was in our pathway, we would pray, and the Lord would remove the obstacles. God is greater than all Mafia forces, and we knew that no matter what they tried to do to us, they would have to contend with the King. The glory I experienced being with the Lord in intimacy, and the endless life in front of me was worth the tribulation and the trials.

Feeding the Poor

While I was attending church in Alpharetta, I felt God telling me to give bread to his people who attended the church on Sundays. Now my pastor had asked me not to bring bread for the poor inside the church. I would leave the service early on Sundays, load the bread into the trunk of my car, and pass it out in the parking lot. As people left the church, they took the food. I had been doing that for a few months, trusting in the Lord and feeling like I was in obedience to him.

One day, a couple came up to me in tears. They told me that one of them had been unemployed for a few months. The husband said that if it had not been for the food waiting for them at the church, they would have starved. They had a nice car, and on the outside, everything looked just great, but the man went on to say they were literally living off the weekly food we gave them, and he could never thank me enough. I was so excited to be used by God and amazed at how he cared for his people.

A visitor at the church gave me a word from the Lord. Through him, the Lord told me that he would take me places no man could take me. He said, "You are my bride."

The Lord told me he had given me faith to move mountains. At that time, I told the Lord in my heart that I would like a ring.

Give Her the Check

One day, I gave some of the donated food to a woman and her children who were living in a trailer park. The children were delighted to receive the food. They were obviously very needy, and while I was inside her home, the Lord told me to write her a check for $250. I only had $300 in the bank myself, so when I thought about it, I said, "Lord, I am in the same shape as this woman. I cannot believe you would ask me to take most of my money and give it to this lady."

I went home, but I could not get that thought out of my mind. God put it on my heart over and over to give her a check, so I drove back the next day. I walked into her trailer and said, "God told me to give you this money."

She turned her head to the children and exclaimed, "I told you God would come through!" What I did not know was that they were about to be evicted. That amount of $250 was exactly what they needed to remain in their home. You could see the excitement in their little faces. They began to glorify God continuously for his provision, and my heart was broken. I was so thankful in that moment that the Lord could use me to be the hand of God.

In the bread ministry, the Lord taught me to listen to his Spirit. I would drive through the trailer parks and listen to the Lord as to where he would have me stop and open up my trunk.

This was my training in moving by the Spirit and in hearing his voice.

One day, God told me to get out of the car and take a flat of food to the top of the stairs of an apartment building. I obediently stopped and went up the stairs. When I got to the top and knocked on the door, a man opened it, and I was shocked to see that the entire apartment was bare. There was no furniture in sight and certainly no food. I reached over the doorway and said to the man, "God told me to give this to you." The man immediately started weeping and took the food. I was gloriously praising God as I walked back down the steps. He is hope to the hopeless.

Mary Healed of Cancer

One day, I stopped in another park and met a woman named Mary. She was mentally slow, and so was her boyfriend. Mary had a huge lump on her belly, and she told me she had been diagnosed with seven different types of cancer. The last time she visited the doctors, they told her not to return because there was no longer any hope for her, that she was going to die. But I told her, "Go get your son, and we are going to pray, because my God is a healer. He never says there is no hope." We got into a circle and prayed.

Mary was excited when she called me the next day and told me, "I don't know what's going on, but the lump on my stomach is gone!" Later that week, Mary went to see her doctors, and they were astounded. The test results had improved, and the lump had gotten smaller.

Mary laughed and said they even bought a new machine to check her with. During the next few weeks, the same doctors that had told her to not return now wanted her in their offices all the time. Before her next visit, they even wanted her to write down everything she was eating. Every time they tested her, the cancer was smaller and smaller. She would call me often to tell me about the doctors' questions and reactions, and each time, I told her to tell them, "It is Jesus Christ who heals."

The Mafia's Assignment Is finished

After about a year and a half of distributing bread, we were getting donations of food from all over. My garage was always loaded with bread. I had so much bread that other churches were coming to pick up the donations at my place and even help with the distribution. We had become a warehouse distributor of bread for the needy.

Morning after morning, I would meet with the King. One morning, I heard the audible voice of God speaking a blessing over me. When he spoke, my body melted. It felt like life was shooting through me. I meditated on the Ruler of the Universe being there in my room and speaking blessings over me. It was wonderful—like a magnificent dream.

Another morning, he appeared in a burning bush. I met with the Lord daily, and it was always an exciting, new, and glorious adventure. His touch, his look into your eyes, and his purpose for your life is so much greater than you can imagine. God will pick you up in his hand and carry you into heavenly places. He will sing over you. His desire is for you to know him. Not just about him, but to know him—the King. I understood what the Apostle Paul meant when he declared this glorious statement in the book of Philippians:

that I may know him and the power of his resurrection, and the fellowship of his sufferings, being conformed to his death,

Philippians 3:10 (NKJV)

Oh, that I may know this King! My spirit cried, "Oh, that I may know him and, oh, that he may know me!"

Not long after this incident, I was lying on my bed, and in a vision, I saw God pick up huge garden shears and cut a lot of wires. I was full of the love of God, and I was not afraid of anything or anyone anymore. In my heart, I knew from this vision that the Mafia's assignment against my son and I was finished. I went downstairs a few hours later and saw a white van in front of my house. As I walked outside, a man got out of the unmarked van, threw a football in the air, and said, "Touchdown." Then he began taking off the surveillance wires that were on my home. I knew on that day that I was free. "God, you were so good to me, and I will forever bless your name."

I had a lot of dreams and visions, so I kept a diary of them. In one of my dreams, there was a TV pastor sitting in a beautiful office. I walked into his office, and there was a big desk of fiery wood. I said, "Pastor, do you mind sharing this office?"

He told me, "No, have a seat."

That was when I knew that I was going to be on television one day and that God had many great plans for me. I was so expectant and excited about what God was going to do with my life that it was hard to contain myself at times.

Wales

We could not have been happier living in our house near Atlanta, Georgia. The bread ministry was busy, and the Mafia was no longer bothering us. I had daily encounters with the Lord and was trying very hard to obey him. Whatever he asked me to do, I wanted to do it, and quickly. Walking with the Lord was such a great adventure, and I cherished it.

One day, Blake was playing the James Bond 007 game on his Nintendo. When he landed in London, the Lord spoke to him and said, "You and your mom are going to London." When he came into my bedroom and told me, I knew it was from God, and I had an instant witness to what he said. We had very few funds in our bank account, so buying passports could have put our account into overdraft. However, God told us to go the post office and order our US passports, so I obeyed. My roommate at that time did not feel the message was from God. She was afraid the people depending on the bread ministry would starve, but I knew I had heard God's voice. He had told me to follow him, and I was not looking for reasons to disobey.

People around you are often the biggest stumbling blocks. When God wants you to do something, many times, the people around you are not the witness. The key is to be like one of the patriarchs or prophets and respond when he speaks. I felt the favor of God come on us very heavily because we were obedient to the voice or vision of the Lord. Jesus Christ always responded when the Father told him to move. He knew the voice of the Father, and so should we. This comes from being intimate with the Lord and spending time with him.

My sheep hear my voice, and I know them, and they follow me;

John 10:27 (NASB)

Within a day or two, somebody came to my house and gave me a check for $500 as a deposit for the purchase of our motor home. I deposited that check, and our check cleared for the passports. Later, right before we were to buy plane tickets, the people paid us the balance they owed for the motor home. We rented our house in Georgia to some people from the church. We put our treasures in a closet and vowed one day we would return. After all we had been through, it was difficult to leave the safe place called home. We knew that no matter the cost, we were going to obey, and we were excited about what God was going to do with our lives.

I went to tell my pastor that God was calling us to Wales. The pastor made an announcement to the church and said if anyone felt like praying for us, to do so directly. We had no commissioning from our church because God had something better lined up.

Later, right before we were to buy plane tickets, the people paid us the balance they owed for the motor home. Before we left, a friend of our pastor said he was speaking in Swansea, Wales, and I felt Swansea would be a good starting place for us. From Swansea, Blake and I traveled around Wales for ninety days. We blew the shofar and rode trains while we went wherever God told us to go.

It was not an easy journey, but we were so expectant and excited about what God was doing and what he was going to do. We kept looking for God and his signs as we traveled. We may have seemed weird at times to other Christians, and we were not always treated with kindness. I had no church background before my radical encounter with Jesus Christ. The school I was in was with the Spirit, and it was a daily walk. I knew the Lord was teaching me how to follow him. Whatever he said, I just did it. I did not question why or what. I obeyed unconditionally and loved God with all my heart.

Blake was having many dreams and encounters with the Lord too. One night, he told me about heaven opening up, and the Lord handing him the sword of David. Blake could hear the voice of God and see in the spirit. I asked Blake, "How do you know it is God's voice?"

He said, "Mom, I hear the Lord like I hear you. It is like music in my ears."

Many nights, he would wake up and talk about heaven.

The Lord asked him one day when he was sitting in heaven with him if he would like a drink. Blake said, "Yes, Lord," and immediately, a drink appeared in front of him. Blake said, "Mom, God only has to think about something, and it happens." The Lord showed Blake many things about heaven. He met Noah and his family along with Samson and many others. Blake said to me, "Samson was so full of love." Samson had sinned greatly against the Lord. The Lord restored him, and he finished the race. Samson was forgiven much, and God says the ones who are forgiven much are full of love. I am one of those people who have been forgiven much, and I can feel the transforming love of God flowing through me.

> For this reason I say to you, her sins, which are many, have been forgiven, for she loved much; but he who is forgiven little, loves little."
>
> Luke 7:47 (NASB)

Blake told me one night, "Mom, when I went to sleep, the Lord was holding me. When I woke up, he was still holding me." We were so blessed at the tenderness and care of the Lord. His love overwhelmed us daily.

Commissioning

Two days before I left for Florida, an elder from the same church called me and said, "I have been up all night. Before you came to our church a year and a half ago, the elders had a meeting. We asked God to give us an outreach to the poor. You showed up with the bread ministry to the poor, but we didn't realize that you were the answer to our prayer. God woke me up last night and said that you were our answer, and he told me we are to take over your bread ministry."

The church took over the bread ministry, and twenty volunteers signed up right away. I was very happy they had honored what God had begun. In my spirit, I knew the favor of God would be upon them as they ministered to the poor.

We returned to Florida to visit my mom and dad before leaving for the mission field in Wales. Back in Florida, and before I left for Wales again, I was very blessed by Solid Rock Church and Recovery Center. My spiritual mother, Glenda, who was part of the church, said she was going to talk to the pastors and have us commissioned. She said, "Let me talk with our pastor and see if we can lay hands on you." Glenda added, "We must give you a proper send-off to the mission field." This sounded so wonderful and official. I was so excited and expectant to be commissioned as a missionary for God. I had been chosen by God in the heavens to be one of his sent ones.

The Solid Rock Church and Recovery Center in St. Petersburg, Florida, was full of recovering addicts, homeless, and down and outs. Solid Rock organized a going-away party for me in one of their services. People brought me a jar of pennies, a pair of nylons, and a few pencils as gifts to go to the mission field. Now, to the general church, that small offering would not have looked like much, but to the Lord, it was a treasure because it was all they could afford to offer. After they gave their gifts to me, they prayed for me and began to cry. The people were so honored and said, "We never dreamed God would give our church a missionary. For God to give us an international missionary is beyond anything we could have ever dreamed. We are going to pray for you every week."

Every week while I was in Wales, they would interrupt their service to pray for me and blow the shofar. I will never forget the launch to the nations from those most honorable ones.

The Ring

Pastor Karen Dunham

The pastor let me preach on Sunday, which was a very big honor at Solid Rock Church. When I finished my message, a Vietnam veteran came up to me and seemed embarrassed when he said, "You are going to think this is crazy, but God told me to buy you a wedding ring."

I told him I did not think it was crazy because I had prayed and asked God for a ring. We arranged to go out and buy a ring, which I still have on my hand today.

I love his breath blowing upon me. The gentleness of his voice is like rain sprinkling upon you. To be the bride of the King of the Universe, forever his, is a great calling. It is for anyone that will take the leap of faith and say yes to the King. His love for his bride is very deep and beyond expression. It is like love washing over you with waves. When he gives you a taste of his love, everything and everyone around you is beautiful. When his life floods your body, it is all you care about. A new way of living in Jesus Christ is the highest prize.

Preaching in the Streets

This time, when I arrived in Wales, we settled in a small town north of Swansea. The church we attended was small and religious. I felt God calling me to preach in the streets of Wales, so street preacher John and I went to Swansea and teamed up with a group of elderly street preachers outside Saint Mary's every Saturday. They had a little portable amplifier, and each would take turns preaching for ten minutes with the microphone. The group had been meeting together for about thirty years, and I was honored to be with them.

Those preachers were a totally different type of preacher than anyone I had ever met. They were from different backgrounds, churches, and denominations, yet they were unified in the Spirit. They were faithful and would be preaching in the streets every week until they died. I remember one old man named Albert, who was out there preaching the week before he died. He was in his late seventies or eighties. One day, they announced that Albert was with the Lord. He was such an inspiration. No matter how sick he was or how cold it was, Albert would give it a go when it was his turn to preach.

One day, they invited me to a prayer meeting to hear missionaries who were visiting Swansea. The first man who got up testified that forty years ago, missionaries went to the jungles of Africa to preach the gospel. He went on to say that he was the fruit of that labor and was now working for the Lord.

The second man was Asian and said that his mission had failed. He had started a church, found a piece of land, and stayed in prayer. The congregation continuously fasted and prayed for a church to be built on the property. Instead, another group came in and bought the property and built a church. The missionary felt like the mission failed, but the Lord told me it was a success. All the man's prayers were answered; he just could not see it. There has never been a prayer prayed to the Lord that went unheard—never.

Sometimes on Friday afternoons, we would stand outside the mosque at about two o'clock and wait for the men to finish praying. My friend Edna and I would hand out Bibles to the people on their way out of the mosque.

One day, instead of going to Saint Mary's, I felt the Lord wanted me to go to the city center. I told the other preachers, and they were overly joyous. They felt the Lord was expanding their ministry. So there we were in the city center. I stood outside, preaching in the same area for around six months with a little amplifier. I would play some music on the amp and then preach for about ten to fifteen minutes. Then I would hand out gospel tracts while the music played. We had different lines for people who wanted us to pray for them. We had lines for blessings, for healings, and for giving your life to Jesus Christ.

God Taking Me through Death

Garden Tomb Jerusalem

My spiritual journey was incredible during this time. My quiet times with the Lord were intense and wonderful. The Lord began talking to me and asking me if I would die for him. I did not fully understand what he meant at the time. I thought at first that maybe I would literally die, like be hit by a train or something.

Then God told me to fast only with water. I fasted for so long that I lost count of the days.

> For to be carnally minded is death, but to be spiritually minded is life and peace. Because the carnal mind is enmity against God; for it is not subject to the law of God, nor indeed can be. So then, those who are in the flesh cannot please God.
>
> Romans 8:6–8 (NKJV)

The Bible refers to the carnal mind as the old man. Near the beginning of the fast, the Lord gave me a vision of him killing the old man. The old man was a stinking fat walrus, and the Lord struck it with his sword until it was dead. That was the first part of my death process.

My son, Blake, got very sick during that time of fasting and was running a very high fever. His temperature was so high that his eyes were swollen. I went to the store to buy him some juice, and when I got back, I was amazed to find him awake. Blake said, "When you left, the Lord told me to get up and take Communion." He cried as he told me, "The Lord promised me by morning I would be healed." The next morning, he was healed.

I had been fasting for over forty days when the Lord told me to stop drinking water too. At that time, I was a size zero. If I did not stay tuned into the Spirit of the Lord, I would fall down every time I stood up and tried to walk. But as long as I was in the Spirit, I could walk and talk. That was a great spiritual exercise for me that taught me how to stay in the Spirit. I truly knew I was dead. I had not stepped outside of my house in weeks. I had the fear of the Lord on me and was afraid of God.

> Knowing, therefore, the terror of the Lord, we persuade men; but we are well known to God, and I also trust are well known in your consciences.
>
> 2 Corinthians 5:11 (NKJV)

I was on a no-food-or-water fast. and God said, "If you take a drink, it will cost you everything." I felt the anguish of death. I would put a wet rag on my head, and it would give me about two seconds of relief. I was lying on my bed, and the next thing I knew, I was on the cross. I was on the cross with my hands nailed, and there was rope around my wrists. I was dying, and life was seeping out of me. I was in such anguish; I could feel all of it. It was like torture. I was at Calvary, even though I had never been to Jerusalem. I am not sure how long this lasted, but it felt like days. Then all of a sudden, I was dead. I know that if an ambulance would have come to my house right then, and they had taken my pulse, they would have pronounced me dead. After that, I heard the Father say audibly, "Cut him down." I felt my body physically fall to the ground. Then the Lord Jesus Christ picked me up and lay me in a tomb.

A day or two later, God told me I could drink water and eat a small plate of watermelon. I was crying in thankfulness because he had given me a plate of food. I kept pleading with Jesus Christ to let me experience the resurrection. I did not want to stay in the tomb. This is the scripture he gave me.

> Jesus said to her, "I am the resurrection and the life; he who believes in me will live even if he dies, and everyone who lives and believes in me will never die. Do you believe this?"
>
> John 11:25–26 (NASB)

I understand today that he is the resurrection when we are in union with him, As we die daily to ourselves, we allow him to live his resurrected life in and through us. The greater the surrender, the greater the power of God manifests in and through you. To be crucified with Christ, as Paul says in Galatians 2:20, is to let him live his life totally in and through you. It is no longer your life but his.

Swansea, Wales

Feeling the call to preach on the streets, I moved down to Swansea and teamed up with those elderly street preachers outside Saint Mary's every Saturday. They had a little portable amplifier, and each would take turns preaching for ten minutes with the microphone. The group had been meeting together for about thirty years, and I was honored to be with them.

Sometimes on Friday afternoons, we would stand outside the mosque at about two o'clock and wait for the men to finish praying. My friend Edna and I would hand out Bibles to the people on their way out of the mosque.

One day, instead of going to Saint Mary's, I felt the Lord wanted me to go to the city center. I told the other preachers, and they were overly joyous. They felt the Lord was expanding their ministry. So there we were in the city center. I stood outside, preaching in the same area for around six months with a little amplifier. I would play some music on the amp and then preach for about ten to fifteen minutes. Then I would hand out gospel tracts while the music played. We had different lines for people who wanted us to pray for them. We had lines for blessings, for healings, and for giving your life to Jesus Christ.

Standing in the Steps of John Wesley

Someone on the street came up to me one day and asked, "Do you know you are standing where John Wesley preached?" Of course, I had no idea, so they took me over to a plaque next to where I had been preaching every week that said, "John Wesley, Field Preacher."

Wesley is known for great open-air campaigns, where he preached the need for personal holiness and God's great answer to our need for sanctification. The resulting Holiness movement was a major influence in the life of William Seymour, the Azusa Street Revival, and early Pentecostalism.

John Wesley is the founder of the Methodist church. I thought, *Wow, God, John Wesley must have also heard you say to stand in this spot and preach hundreds of years ago.* I was so amazed and in awe at everything I heard God say. God speaks, and he will show you the way.

Two thousand people passed through the city center of Swansea every day. Blake was around thirteen or fourteen at that time, and he loved to skateboard. He was with me in the city center. He was skateboarding with his friends as I was preached. The Goth kids were also skateboarding in the city center. Some wore chains and had their hair dyed black. Those kids would harass my son because I was a preacher.

One day, God told me to preach, "God did not create any mistakes. No matter how fat or thin you are, no matter what you look like, God did not make a mistake. You have a destiny and a purpose. No matter what men have said to you, your family, or anyone else, God did not create any mistakes."

One of Blake's friends, Sean, made his way up to the front. He said, "All my life I have been told that I was no good for anything by my mother. I have tried to commit suicide a couple times, and this morning, I tried again by taking a lot of pills. I just don't know what to do anymore." The only thing I knew to do was to tell him to put his finger down his throat and throw up while we lay hands on him and prayed.

As we prayed for him, many of the kids gathered around to watch as Sean vomited a large pile of pills onto the ground. As the kids watched how we cared for the boy, the Lord kept him alive. We lay Sean on a bench and continuously prayed and encouraged him.

From that day on, something changed. Those young Goth kids became our armor bearers. When the local drunks tried to run us off, the Goth kids would get up and tell them to leave us alone. It was magnificent to have them hanging around us and listening to the gospel.

Every Saturday, from one to six in the afternoon, we had a good-sized crowd. They were coming and going while we had church in the streets. People would get on trains from other areas of Wales to come to the church meeting in the streets. I would preach for about ten to fifteen minutes and then pass the microphone to others who were attending our home service. Sometimes, the students from Swansea Bible College would preach with us too. We played music, handed out gospel tracts, and prayed with people. The Lord continuously gave us souls and made us fruitful.

In Jesus's Name, Stop Raining!

One Saturday, as I was preaching, it started to rain. Several of the kids were outside skateboarding with Blake. Normally, when it rained, we would pack up and move the sound equipment to a shelter, but this time, God told me to leave the amplifier on, even though it was starting to sprinkle. God then told me he was going to stop the rain and that I needed to tell the people to stay.

Some of the people laughed and walked away. The Goth kids were under a tree for shelter, saying to Blake, "Look at what your mom is saying over there." I was waiting for God to do what he had promised. It was raining steadily now, but the Lord told me, "Do it like I told you."

I said, "The Lord rebuke you, rain!" I shouted, "In Jesus's name, stop raining! The Lord commands you to stop!"

The rain that was in midair immediately stopped. It was amazing to everyone, and I personally was amazed at what God had done.

Blake's friends, along with the Goth kids, were all over Blake, saying, "Your mom is the greatest! Did you see what God just did for your mother? I wish my mom was doing great things like that."

Blake loved and needed every moment of encouragement. Blake came home that afternoon and said, "Mom, you can preach anytime you want in the streets. I am so proud of you, and so are my friends."

The Lord will vindicate you every time and give you a table before your enemies. Just trust in God and watch what he does on your behalf.

Into the Fountain

On another Saturday, we were out in the street, preaching. The day was special for rugby fans because it was one of the all-time rugby matches. A crowd was gathered inside a bar to watch the game. I was standing outside the bar at my regular spot at the top of the amphitheater with my loud speaker. On that day, instead of preaching my normal ten to fifteen minutes, the Spirit of the Lord was on me to keep preaching. The place where I stood in the city center had a police camera that monitored my every move. The people inside the bar were heckling me and telling me to stop, but I just kept preaching.

Eventually, the men came out of the bar and picked me up with my microphone in hand. My microphone was not very good quality, and it broke as they carried me toward the fountain in the city center. I yelled at my friend, "Guard the amp!" I was holding onto my Bible, and the men were holding me up in the air. I was looking up at the clouds as they carried me through the air. I felt in my heart that God was not going to let anything happen to me. I was waiting for lightning to hit the men. They carried me over to the fountain and threw me into the water. I was surely humbled as I came out of the water.

The police came running out to me. They said they had it all on tape, and they were going to go arrest those men. I said, "No, God did not send me here to put people in jail." I went down the block, bought a new microphone, and started preaching again. The next Saturday, as I was preaching outside the same bar as usual, I saw that those men's hearts had changed. God had performed a miracle. They were coming up to me in little groups and apologizing. They were standing around, listening to me preach. They sat down with their beers, listened to me preach, and asked questions about Jesus Christ. It was so wild and wonderful and so like God. Not long after that day, the bar closed down, but I was still out there preaching every Saturday.

Deliverance of Brent

An amazing deliverance happened to a young friend of Blake's named Brent. Brent showed up at my door one morning, when he was supposed to be in school. As he came in, I asked him what he needed.

"Ma'am, I have to tell you s-something." Brent shuffled his feet. "One day, when I was leaving school, there was this man who picked me up in his car. He, he…" His voice trailed off, and when he finally looked up from the floor where he'd kept his gaze the whole time, what I saw in his eyes made me want to hug him.

Brent kept on, " I just keep thinking about it. I want to stop. I want to get it out of my head, but I just can't. I don't know why I didn't just jump out of the car or run away. Just scared I guess."

Brent was desperate, and my heart broke for him. I told him, "Jesus Christ can do what no doctor can do. Let me pray for you, Brent." As I began to pray for him, the power of God came upon this boy. The presence of God was all over him, and the shame lifted off of him as I explained that there is no condemnation in Jesus Christ. The blood of the Lamb of God washes us clean. We must forgive those who have abused us, or our hate will destroy us. Brent let the Spirit of God take the spiritual stronghold off him. After a few minutes, with tears and smiles, I knew he had been delivered. The sweetness of being free is the blessing for those that come to Jesus Christ for help. The spiritual bricks were no longer on his shoulders.

While Brent was getting ready to leave, he said, "For my whole life, I have been going to all kinds of doctors and counseling, but none of them could help me. After just fifteen minutes with Jesus Christ I feel great!" And he walked out the door.

Home Church Glory

The home church meeting in Swansea Wales

In addition to street preaching in Swansea, we had a small home church going. Our little church had a reputation for being a deliverance ministry. People used to say that when they walked up the stairs to the apartment, by the time they reached the top of the second story, they could feel the cloud of the Holy Spirit.

One night, a woman showed up at our meeting. We asked her where she was from and who told her about us, but she would not answer. The woman was hunched over, and she looked years older than she was. I told the team, "Let's lay hands on her and find out what we can see in the Spirit."

We began praying for the legions of demons to come off of her. Two of the members of our team were Chris and a widow named Carol. I said, "Why don't we ask the Lord for a vision to see if she has any more demons on her."

Then the woman began to speak, "They are right here on my shoulder."

We asked the Lord to cast those demons off her. Next, I heard the Lord say, "Pray the words of men off her."

I said, "Lord, we ask that the words of men be removed in Jesus's name, amen. In Jesus's name, free her from the words of men spoken over her life."

The woman was screeching. Then as her body straightened, she stood up. She told us her name was Janet. She asked, "What year is it?" We said it was 2002, and she said, "Twenty years ago, I was injected with drugs and put into a mental institution. I have been in prison ever since." Then Janet started to praise God! As she was leaving, she said, "The doctors are never going to believe this." She walked out of there a completely transformed woman.

Through this experience, the Lord taught me about deliverance from the power of the words of men. People destroy one another with words and do not understand the power of words. The weight of the words of doctors telling her she would never be free from mental illness, people calling her crazy, and the powerful drugs had kept this precious daughter bound all those years.

> Death and life are in the power of the tongue, and those who love it will eat its fruit.
>
> (Proverbs 18:21 (NASB)

Apostle Roy

One of the members of our home church was Roy. He was very angry because for seven years, he tried to get deliverance, but no one could help him get free. Roy had gone from church to church for help. In addition to preaching on the streets with us, Roy would come to our home meetings. On the street, this man was a great preacher.

At that point in my spiritual life, I was alone with God from nine in the morning until two in the afternoon. Every day, I wanted to saturate myself with the presence of God. I would listen to the word of God day and night. One morning, God gave me a vision of him walking to the end of a fishing pier. Roy was swimming around the pier in black water. Then there was a light that shone down on him from heaven. When God got to the end of the pier, he said, "Apostle." I knew God wanted to ordain Roy as an apostle.

A couple of meetings later, I told Carol and Chris to be ready. Then we prophesied over Roy and told him, "God said you are an apostle." We anointed Roy's head with oil, prayed for him, and everyone blessed him according to the vision of the Lord.

It did not seem to be very long at all (maybe ten days later) when Carol said, "Look at Roy." Everyone in the group looked at Roy. Everything about Roy had changed. He was not walking the same, he was not talking the same, and even the way he held himself was different. Everything about him had changed. I thought, *Wow God!* When the prophetic word is made sure, and destiny comes upon you, you launch. There is no mountain that can keep you from coming into destiny. We were all so blown away at what God had done right before our eyes. The word of God had transformed Roy into an apostle. Roy walked in deliverance and freedom and rejoiced at serving the Lord.

While I was in Wales, my church back home, Solid Rock Church, sent me an e-mail. They were still praying for me every week. At one of their prayer meetings, God told them to ordain me as a pastor when I came home. I was so honored by this. When I got home, they ordained me. They cried over me and licensed me as a pastor. I had questions, and the Lord showed me a lot about this. I loved it when he said, "It is not about you, but it is me inside of you doing the work." He taught me not to limit him, as he can do anything the Father shows him to do. He lives his life in and through this crucified body of mine. His promise is that he will carry me to the finish line and into the endless life.

> I am crucified with Christ: nevertheless I live; yet not I, but Christ liveth in me: and the life which I now live in the flesh I live by the faith of the son of God, who loved me, and gave himself for me.
>
> Galatians 2:20 (KJV)

Samuel Howells

Rev. Samuel Howells and Karen Dunham

Rev. Samuel Howells and his secretary Ruth

Before I went to Wales, I had read Rees Howells's book on intercession. Rees Howells was Welsh. The ministry and Bible college he founded in Swansea was still active when I arrived. I knew I had to be in Swansea, Wales, and I had to find Samuel Howells, Rees's son.

I had a very strong desire to walk in the mantle of intercession. On my first visit, I made an appointment to go alone to Reverend Samuel. Later, I came back with a group of visitors from my church in Clydach. I was allowed to visit him several times, even though his secretary used to say she did not know how I was able to get those appointments because he did not like to see anyone. Ruth said, "Samuel says it takes him out of the presence of God to have visitors." He said yes to seeing me every time.

I had never heard anyone preach like Samuel Howells. He used the word of God and flowed in the Spirit so beautifully. My heart would be split open by the time he read the second or third passage of a message. I knew one day, I would preach like him, steady in the stream.

One time, in a private meeting with Rev. Samuel Howells, I knew by faith that I wanted him to lay hands on my head and pray for me. Reverend Samuel was in his black suit and bow tie. I asked him, "What was it like when your father gave you away?"

He said, "Living with my uncle was good. They treated me well."

Then I asked him, "Samuel, why did you never marry?"

He said, "Get married? I gave my life to the Lord." When he told me how the Lord made full restoration between him and his father upon his return from Africa, I wept. I fell on my knees before this eighty-year-old conservative man and said, "I know you have prayed the mantle of intercession onto me a couple of times, and I know the glory of the Lord has fallen on me. But I feel you are to lay hands on my head and pray again." Samuel put his hands on my head and prayed with such glorious power. I felt the Lord drop a mantle onto me that day for intercession.

> Therefore he is able also to save forever those who draw near to God through him, since he always lives to make intercession for them.
>
> Hebrews 7:25 (NASB)

Oh, how he lives to make intercession, and how I wanted to please the Lord in this holy union he had brought me into. I wanted to swim in his love, be clothed in his mantles, and move in his gifting. Whatever God had, I wanted it all. To know the King and be known by him was always on my mind.

Double Portion of the Spirit in Israel

Karen Dunham Jordan River Israel

Through an invitation from Samuel Howells, I was able to take my first trip to Israel with the Swansea Bible College. The country of Israel had issued the team a special invitation, and most of the trip was sponsored. Tourism at that time, in 2001, was very low in Israel because of the political situation. Our team was very excited for me to go to Israel. They said, "You must get in the Jordan River when you go to Israel, and God will give you a double portion of the Spirit." I asked the pastor who was leading the tour if I could get into the Jordan River, and he agreed.

When I arrived in the promised land, it was like being in a dream. Being in Israel was an awesome experience! This is the land that the Lord our God cares for. His eye is always on it. It drinks the rain of heaven.

> But the land into which you are about to cross to possess it, a land of hills and valleys, drinks water from the rain of heaven, a land for which the LORD your God cares; the eyes of the LORD your God are always on it, from the beginning even to the end of the year.
>
> Deuteronomy 11:11–12 (NASB)

When we got to the Jordan River, I reminded the pastor that he promised I could go into the water. The other students were not going in because of religious reasons. I had not talked to many of them about getting a double portion of the Spirit, as I did not want anyone to talk me out of meeting with the Lord in the River. The pastor was not going to baptize anyone on this trip, so I asked Roy, who was also from our Wales team, to baptize me. As I went under into the water, I felt so thankful to the Lord for his glorious promises. As I stepped out of the river, our Jewish guide, Aaron, said, "I want to read something to you." He began reading the following passage over me:

> The Spirit of the Lord GOD is upon me, because the LORD has anointed me to preach good tidings to the poor; He has sent me to heal the brokenhearted, to proclaim liberty to the captives, and the opening of the prison to those who are bound; to proclaim the acceptable year of the LORD, and the day of vengeance of our God; to comfort all who mourn, to console those who mourn in Zion, to give them

beauty for ashes, the oil of joy for mourning, the garment of praise for the spirit of heaviness; that they may be called trees of righteousness, the planting of the LORD, that he may be glorified. And they shall rebuild the old ruins, they shall raise up the former desolations, and they shall repair the ruined cities, the desolations of many generations. Isaiah 61:1–4 (NKJV)

My heart exploded as Aaron said, "Do you know this is in the Bible twice?" He flipped the pages to Luke and read over me again:

The Spirit of the LORD is upon Me, because He has anointed me to preach the gospel to the poor; He has sent me to heal the brokenhearted, to proclaim liberty to the captives and recovery of sight to the blind, to set at liberty those who are oppressed; to proclaim the acceptable year of the LORD.

Luke 4:18–19 (NKJV)

I was totally amazed at the Lord when he gave me such a great confirmation of the double portion of his spirit. It was a dream to have those blessings in the Scriptures read over me as I came out of the Jordan River. The tour guide did not know Jesus Christ, but he surely knew the scripture and was used mightily by the Lord to release the blessing over me.

God is so great, and wow, he will make it happen for you if you keep your eyes upon him. He can do the impossible and loves to use his mighty power to show himself strong on your behalf.

Carol and Chris

Part of my team in Swansea consisted of two good friends, Chris and Carol. I met both of them during my first year in Wales. Chris was a homeless fellow living on the streets, who used to come to pray with us. Carol was someone that would go to church, but no one wanted to spend time with her. She was a very needy person. While I was still in Clydach, Carol's husband died, and she asked me if I would be one of the pastors to come pray at her husband's funeral. She could not pray because she was still mourning her husband's death.

Not long after I met her, the Lord told me that she was to be the prayer partner I had been praying for. I taught her on the two topics I knew a lot about, which were fasting and intimacy. Carol got serious about fasting for the Lord, and she lost one-hundred twenty-five pounds. This seemed to happen overnight. She had a heavy anointing of God upon her. I learned so much from her about seeing in the Spirit.

One time, there was a missing boy in the city, and God gave her a vision of exactly where he was. She told the police, and they went to the abandoned building and found the boy. Moving in the gifts of God is fantastic.

Now when she went to church, people would come around her and ask for prayer. She was also the most loving woman with the biggest heart of mercy. She would cry over people while praying. We had a man, who had been living in a dumpster for months, come in off the street. He had rat bites all over his body, and his feet were in terrible condition. Carol removed his shoes and then cleaned and anointed his feet. She ministered to this man who was covered with rat bites and infections with love that made me cry. It did not matter to Carol who the people were; she loved them all.

Carol was so dramatically transformed that people would frequently come up to ask me how long she had been in our ministry. They wanted to know what I had been teaching her. It was amazing how fast God had taken her into his glorious chambers of love. It was like the Spirit of God camped out on this precious saint.

In our home church meetings during the week, Chris and Carol would always be there. They were both amazing people of God. They handed out a lot of gospel tracts and led people to Jesus Christ on an individual basis more than anyone else I had met. We would put all our coins together every day and buy more gospel tracts. We were having such an outbreak of the Holy Spirit in our street ministry that a newspaper did an article about us. They called it "Queue Up for a Modern-Day Miracle."

Miracles in the Streets

A Baptist minister from a local church came one day and asked for prayer for his church. I said, "Let me pray for you now." As I went to pray for him, God put him on the ground and pinned him there. The Spirit was so heavy on the man that he could not even move, and he began weeping. The whole time, he was saying, "I do not even believe in this sort of thing." I told him to just stay there and let the Lord minister to him.

The people got into lines based on what they needed. We had one for prayer, one for blessing, one for healing, and one for salvation. In the healing and blessing lines, we handed out hankies with scriptures on them that we had prayed over. We saw amazing manifestations and healings from those hankies. One ten-year old that we had prayed for said, "Please let me have a hankie for my mother because she is sick." We gave him one, and the next week, he came back and said, "I just wanted to tell you that as soon as my mom put the hankie on her head, her headache went away." It was such a joy to hear about testimonies of what God can and is willing to do.

> God was performing extraordinary miracles by the hands of Paul, so that handkerchiefs or aprons were even carried from his body to the sick, and the diseases left them and the evil spirits went out.
>
> Acts 19:11–12 (NASB)

Put Out of the Ministry

During that time, Carol, Chris, and I were learning so much about intimacy with Jesus. We were growing deep relationships with one another and with the Lord. Carol and Chris told me they were in love and wanted to get married. Carol was a widow in her fifties, and Chris was in his twenties.

Local pastors started coming to me and saying that I would have to put Chris and Carol out of the ministry if they did not stop making plans to get married. They told me Chris was previously engaged to another widow and that the pastor had broken it off. Prior to this, those pastors had never said much to me.

I sat down with Chris and Carol and told them I could not provide them with gospel tracts anymore. I told them they could no longer be involved with Living Bread if they married. When I told them this, it absolutely broke them into pieces. They told me later that they felt so bad that they wanted to take their Bibles and throw them in a dumpster. They had served the Lord with everything they had in their hearts. They had won so many souls, and now to be treated like this was devastating. It crushed them completely.

As their spiritual leader, it was a mistake on my part to have listened to the words of men. Even though Carol and Chris are divorced today, I should have handled it all with love that never fails, rather than listening to the religious. What a huge lesson I learned about the mercies of the Lord and his love for his people even in their broken condition.

9/11

In 2001, Blake and I left Wales and traveled to the United States to visit my family. When we returned to Wales a month later, we were on a flight from New York to London. The 9/11 attacks on America happened that same morning while we were in the air. I had fallen asleep on the plane, and all of a sudden I had sweat all over my body. In a dream, I saw planes crashing and going down. I was screaming, "Give your lives to Jesus!" When I woke up, I had the fear of God and water on my face. The dream was so real that I was wondering if I was supposed to scream, not knowing if the plane I had seen was the one I was on. I was looking all around at the people near me, trying to figure out if I had seen them in my dream or not. I did not know that planes were going down in New York while I was having that dream.

When we landed in London, everything had changed. I got ready to go through passport control to enter the country and then pass through to Wales. Normally, this was just a formality, but now it was an interrogation. They were drilling everyone because we were getting off a plane from New York. Prior to my visit home, I had spoken with a British immigration officer about obtaining a missionary visa. He told me I could get a stamp when I came through from America. I told the officer at passport control this information, but the man would not listen to me. I pleaded with him and said all my things were in my house in Wales. He gave us permission to enter for one month and said we could appeal his decision at the local office in Swansea. Our passports were stamped in black. I did not know it meant we had been refused entry. We got a month of grace from the officer to go to our home.

One month later, on October 11, my birthday, I went to the appeals office. When I got there, they said I had to leave the country. I was very disappointed. At that point, another missionary was about to come join our ministry. How could this happen now after all the work we had done for God in this country? I stood outside the office after the appointment and, looking up to heaven, I cried out to God, "Why?"

At that time, people from all around the world were saying that a massive revival was coming to Wales, and the prophets were steadily seeing a move of God for Wales. Prayer houses were gathering for hours to pray for revival in Wales. It seemed like everyone was getting ready for revival while I was being told to leave the country. Revival did not fall in Wales at that time. Later, I had a dream and saw an American on the Titanic trying to dock at Wales. In the dream the ship sank because of pride. I was in a very low place in my soul as we headed back to the United States.

The Shift of Change

After our plane landed in New York, I went to plead for a visa from the British consulate. The answer was no. They asked me if I had ever been refused entry, and I said no. Since they had let me stay in my house for a month, I did not realize the full significance of the black stamp in my passport. I knew I had been told to leave the country, but I thought I would be able to go back. The man screamed at me, telling me that I had been refused entry.

Blake and I went back to my mother's house in Florida. I spent a lot of time praying and seeking the Lord. The Lord finally said, "Whatever you make happen for somebody else, know that the same measure comes back on your own head. Welcome Chris and Carol back into Living Bread Ministry and let them hand out gospel tracts."

> Knowing that whatever good thing each one does, this he will receive back from the Lord, whether slave or free.
>
> Ephesians 6:8 (NASB)

I began calling Chris and Carol. I sent them bottles of anointing oil, as they loved getting gifts like that, and I helped pay for their Gospel tracts. God began to deal with my heart too. He said, "I do not kick people out of my kingdom. Bring the children back to me and continue on your path." So I was in the United States for six months.

After a full reconciliation with Chris and Carol, I got a call from the consulate telling me that I was invited back to the United Kingdom. They sent me a visa, but I did not go back because everything had changed. The Lord had said, "The pathway has changed."

I worked at Solid Rock Recovery Center in Florida on and off for about one year. They gave me an old automobile that was ten or twenty years old. I do not recall ever having such an old car, but I was so thankful to have it. One day, I asked the pastor if I could bring a message into the soup kitchen for the homeless. I was bringing the message on Sunday evenings already, but I thought it would be really nice to bring a message to the homeless men in the soup kitchen. The pastor said I could go ahead. After one of the first messages I delivered, the men got up with tears on their faces. They were cheering and roaring as though they were in a football stadium at the preaching of the gospel. I thought, *This is it, God!* I began praying for their healing, homes, and deliverance.

One day, a man got up and said, "Can I have prayer? Could you just pray for me that the Lord would give me some place to sleep." So, I prayed for him in front of all the people there. A few days later, I asked the men, "Does anyone have a testimony?"

This man walked up to the front. Weeping, he said, "I got prayer the other night, and someone was nice enough to give me a place to sleep in the garage." The man was crying and thanking the Lord. I was so moved, as I realized the glory and pleasure that was coming to the Lord through his testimony.

> In all your ways acknowledge him, and he will make your paths straight.
>
> Proverbs 3:6 (NASB)

The Call to Israel

Ein Gedi Israel

As I was sitting in Solid Rock, I was thinking about my situation. I knew it cost me money every time I walked into the church. With all the broken, homeless, and possessed people, it was a very big job, and the people always had needs. I asked God if someone would ever find Blake and me in a soup kitchen. I thought in our walk with Jesus Christ that someone would surely discover us and confirm we had a call of God on our lives.

Within a week or two, Blake and I were being flown to San Diego. We had been offered an incredible job that included money, a house, a car, and the opportunity for me to speak on television. We were negotiating a contract, and people from Christian TV Station were telling us about their business. They were going to send a small work crew to Israel. I was not going to be part of this team, but every time they mentioned Israel, my heart would stir. I thought it was quite exciting because I had already been to Israel once. My parents said, "No matter what you do, you cannot lose this job." I was in the middle of negotiating the contract, but the Lord was telling me to go home and not sign it.

Back in Florida, my very good friends said that I could not take the job in San Diego. They did not feel the witness in the Spirit when they prayed for me. Debbie and Jeaniece were two of the most powerful prayer warriors who had been praying for Blake and me for a long time. I knew I had to listen to them as ones who had heard from God.

In Wales, I had struggled to get Bible tracts, living off very little, and now I had a job offer working for Jesus that paid an income with many benefits. I told God and these praying women I had nothing in Jerusalem. Yet my heartbeat quickened each time I would think about Jerusalem. Later, I gave in to the Lord's nudging and bought tickets to Tel Aviv for Blake and me.

At that time, in 2003, not many would go to Israel because of the ongoing troubles in Iraq. My family thought I was not thinking clearly because I was going into a war zone in Jerusalem. At that time, my flight with British Airways was cancelled because they had stopped flying to Israel. I did not mention this to my family, as they were already worried. I booked a flight with El Al, the only airline still flying to Israel.

Promised Land

Western Wall and Dome of the Rock Jerusalem

In early 2003, Blake and I moved to Israel. I knew in my spirit that we were supposed to go to Jerusalem and put prayer notes in the Western Wall. When we got to Israel, we rented a room at a convent called Ecce Homo. On occasion, we helped by washing dishes. There were not many staying in the Ecce Homo Convent. It seemed like the streets of Jerusalem were empty.

It also felt like the people on the streets of the Old City hated America for killing Iraqis. I never realized how much the world hated Americans until then. The nuns were also upset with us because we would not buy a gas mask. Everyone was getting ready to die, but I thought if that happened, we would walk around and raise the dead on the streets of Jerusalem. I felt no fear of what was happening in the political arena.

> These signs will accompany those who have believed: in my name they will cast out demons, they will speak with new tongues; they will pick up serpents, and if they drink any deadly poison, it will not hurt them; they will lay hands on the sick, and they will recover.
>
> Mark 16:17–18 (NASB)

I felt a calling in my heart to work with wounded Israeli soldiers, and I got the opportunity to do this immediately. I met a young soldier who had been blown off a bus in a terror explosion. The army was telling him he had to go back to work, but he never wanted to put a uniform on again. They were having him tested for psychological damage because he refused to put on his uniform. We sent out an e-mail and raised money for the young soldier. We gave the donation to him on Sukkot, the Feast of Tabernacles, and his family was extremely thankful. It is amazing how God will find you wherever you are and encourage you with a blessing. God loves using his people to do his will.

About two months went by. Blake and I kept busy giving away gospel tracts on the streets, putting prayer requests in the Western Wall, and helping the nuns wash dishes. This was what God had assigned for us to do.

One day, at the New Gate in Jerusalem, I met a Catholic priest who was different from anyone I had ever met. Father George was spending time with the people talking about Jesus. He was giving away videos and gospel tracts, and I was amazed. He said to me, "Go to Jericho, feed the people, and win the whole city for Jesus." No one had ever told me that I could win a whole city. When I heard those words, I felt the Spirit of the Lord touch my heart heavily, and I knew he had spoken the truth. I felt the call of God come on my life. I went home and told my son that we were moving to Jericho. Blake said, "Oh no, Mom, not Jericho."

I said, "Yes, Jericho."

We went down to visit Jericho and spied out the exceedingly good land. It was extremely hot, and we decided to wait another month.

Bus Explosion

I was invited to pray at Samuel's Mountain, near the town of Gibeah, where the prophet Samuel lived. While I was there, Blake, who was about fourteen years old at the time, was walking up a street in Jerusalem when an Israeli bus exploded right in front of him. He turned to run, but police and Secret Service came out from everywhere and made him go back toward the bus. He said he was very afraid, but then he felt heaven open, and all of a sudden, the fear was gone. When he got back up by the bus, a young soldier collapsed. Blake went over to her, picked her up, and held her until the medics came. Another soldier on the scene was holding a gun and shaking badly. Blake said, "Mom, I was afraid she would shoot." He walked up to her and told her that it was not her time to go. He told her she was still alive and that everything would be all right.

When Blake returned to Ecce Homo, the nuns encouraged him. He cleaned himself up, and they offered him a free dinner. He was covered in black soot and little pieces of glass. I will never forget the kindness of those nuns when Blake really needed some kindness. Not long after this, we went to Jericho.

Moving into Jericho

Jericho Crosswalk

Jericho is said to be the oldest and lowest city in the world. It was the first city that Joshua and Israel conquered after they entered the land. It is where Achan stole the mantle, gold, and silver. Israel stoned him, and his family and called it the valley of Achor. Achor means tribulation. The Lord says he will turn the valley of Achor into a door of hope.

Then I will give her vineyards from there, and the valley of Achor as a door of hope.

Hosea 2:15a (NASB)

Jericho is the point of blessing and the doorway to the land. Like my son Blake, I too had asked the Lord, "Why Jericho?"

The Lord said, "You shall enter through the door of the land."

In 2003, the Israeli Defense Force (Israeli army) checkpoints were on the highest state of alert around Jericho. The city had been given over to Palestinian control years earlier, and no one was allowed in or out of Jericho without permission.

Once I got into Jericho, people were afraid of me. No Americans were allowed in Jericho, and it took hours at the checkpoint and phone calls to higher-ranking officers before we were finally allowed to enter the city. The only woman who would rent a house to me (she was in desperate need of money) was located in one of the refugee camps. We moved into the Ein as-Sultan refugee camp on the north side of Jericho, which borders the ruins of the ancient city. My neighbors came over and said, "We never dreamed we would be living with an American in a Palestinian refugee camp." I had no idea who the people were or what kind of climate I had moved into.

In the fall of 2003, the Israeli army called me and asked, "What are you doing in the refugee camp?"

I said, "We are going to build a church."

They said, "Could you come and see us?"

When I went to the meeting, they asked, "What are you going to do with the followers?"

I said, "God has a plan."

From this initial meeting, we built a good relationship and continued to hold monthly meetings. They wanted to know where our funding came from, what our plans were, and what we were doing in Jericho. Even though many advised me not to, I always answered them truthfully. I told we gave away full Arabic

Bibles as part of our educational program. They said as long as they knew what we were doing, they could help arrange aid and passage through the closed checkpoint.

The Palestinians are in a war. Most have never looked at a Bible, yet they say they believe in the holy books. It is because of what is written in the Bible that the nations are either for or against Israel. The Bible talks about God's covenant with Israel and her right to exist. Many of the Palestinians who have lost their land and their lives have never read what God says in the Bible. It is the justice of God to give Bibles to the Palestinians. The Bible has the answer for everyone. Not reading the Bible is like having a blindfold over your eyes. We can receive great understanding of the plan of God for the promised land and the nations through his word.

Being honest and walking in truth without compromise paid off with the liaison officers of the Israeli army and with the Palestinian governmental authority. They would allow supplies into the city on behalf of our ministry when others had trouble coming across the borders. They would also help our staff and volunteers pass through the checkpoints. The officials helped me obtain permits for Palestinians to go out of Jericho.

At meetings, I was amazed when they told me what a great job I was doing. One of the IDF officers said, "If I personally had a child starving, I do not know what I would do. It is great you are feeding the poor."

Others would shake our hands as we were passing through the checkpoint and say, "Thank you for helping the people." I felt the Lord told me to feed the Palestinians, but my own Zionist friends had rebuked me when I moved to Jericho. Some had said, "Why would God tell you to feed the enemy?"

Yet the IDF encouraged me and told us what a great job we were doing. They were the only ones edifying us at times, except for the Spirit of the Lord. It was amazing, and they made us feel like we were doing something great and cutting edge for God, Israel, and the Palestinians.

Refugees and Death Threats

When Blake was fourteen or fifteen years old, young Arab boys would come to visit us nearly every night in the camp. Blake learned Arabic right away, but no one in Jericho seemed to speak much English, so I began teaching English classes to the refugee children after school.

We did not have a fence around our home, and at times, thirty to forty people crammed into our yard and inside of our house. Stealing from foreigners was common in this culture. The minute we would walk out of the living room, they would go through our drawers or pick up our telephones. They would steal anything. Once, I found them in my bedroom rifling through my purse. I screamed at a young woman and chased her out of the house. The next day, the Lord told me to go to her house and apologize for yelling at her.

One day, Blake arrived at our refugee camp house with a small car that had a broken windshield. Blake said, "The neighbor told me we could use his car to do our grocery shopping." The Palestinians were very loving at times. Then Blake said, "We can only drive the car at night, though."

I asked my son, "Why only at night?"

Blake said, "The neighbor stole it from an Israeli."

I looked across the street, and the neighbor was nodding his head yes and waving to me with a big friendly smile on his face. I wondered if at any minute, someone would come and arrest us. I tried to smile and wave back.

I said, "Blake please take the car back and tell the neighbor thank you so much." Then I said, "Son, we cannot ride around in stolen Israeli cars."

We learned some hard lessons in dealing with the refugees in those early days. The one thing that fueled my love and compassion for them was that they were pitiful and very needy. The Lord said to me, "No matter what they do to you, keep loving them." I felt if I could grow to love those people, God could use me anywhere. They were not always easy to love, but the Spirit made a way.

When the terror alerts were high, the checkpoints closed, and the people were not allowed to come in or go out. Every one suffered when the terrorists caused trouble.

We decided to hold an outreach with food and hundreds of World Mission gospel tracts. I asked some friends in Jerusalem to help with the outreach. We assembled three hundred bags of food with gospel tracts in each one. Then we invited people from all the refugee camps in Jericho to our house. We had people all over the place. My friends were shocked to see all the hungry people.

The mosque found out about the tracts and began to preach against us. They preached over the loud speakers that I should be executed along with my son because we were trying to steal the souls of the people. Then even greater crowds of people would come and say the mosque was preaching against us. They would also say that they had heard on the loud speaker that we had food and wanted to know what we could give them. The more the mosque preached against us, the more people came to us. There were so many people outside our house in the camp that we finally closed the doors and locked ourselves in.

None of us knew a lot about the refugees, and we felt much more comfortable speaking to them through the bars on the windows. This went on for hours. Later, we fenced in the property and put up a gate. All over the city of Jericho the people knew where to go to get aid and learn about Jesus.

A few days later, I got on the roof and blew the shofar at ten o'clock in the morning. I blew it in directions to the north, south, east, and west. The sound carried throughout the refugee camp. A day or two later, people were sitting outside with buckets of rocks. They were continuously throwing stones at our house. A couple of our volunteers were very uneasy as they sat inside and listened to the rocks hitting the window. Another threw hot tar at the house.

The next day, Suleiman, our dear friend, said, "They think you are a converted Jew because you were blowing a shofar."

Praise God, they eventually lost interest in throwing rocks, buts other trials came upon us. I was thinking of all the trials and death threats we were receiving when I said to my son, "Reinhard Bonnke said he was God's third pick for an assignment in the mission field. Reinhard said when he got to heaven, he was going to thank the others as he was so blessed." I thought to myself, *What number are we?*

Blake and I prayed and asked the Lord, "What number are we for Jericho?"

Blake looked at me and said, "Mom, God asked thousands to come."

The Spirit of the Lord hit me in the heart heavily when he spoke. I thought, *Okay Lord, we will stay steady.*

A while later, God spoke through a visitor who said, "When God asked you to go and take a call that thousands have said no to, you walked in a thousandfold increase from God."

I believe this is true. I could feel his power and anointing continuously increasing. No matter what God has asked you to do, no matter how bad the door looks in front of you, keep running toward it. When you say yes to God after others have said no, you walk in a tremendously increased blessing.

The Muslims were rough, but the Christians were cruel to us during our early years in Jericho. We felt like lepers to our own people, and the season when we were exiled to Jericho was most difficult. The Lord rewarded us by pouring out a stream of blessing and his favor, which is still flowing today.

There were a few Christians who were supportive, like that one woman who sent me dolls to give to the refugee children. Those love connections made a big difference to children.

I once visited a women's clinic in the refugee camp. When I entered the examination room, I was stunned. I asked Suleiman, "What is that covering the beds?" Little worms were falling from the ceiling and covering the examination table. I did not want to be in there and immediately ran to the door of the clinic. I cried out to the Lord, "Heal the people, Oh Lord, and they will be healed!" I could not imagine sitting on a bed and waiting for a doctor while worms were falling onto me from the ceiling.

We have so much to thank him for, and that situation made me realize how great the blessings that he has poured out on America are. Later that day, Suleiman's mother came to visit me. She watched me pray for people and heal some who were sick. As one woman received deliverance from the spirit of depression, she asked Suleiman, "Is she a nurse?" He explained to her that I was asking God, and he was healing the people. The family stayed and watched people being healed until the last person went home.

Suleiman's father, who was the sheik, was coming to pick them up at my house. The sheik was the Islamic priest of the local mosque. When he arrived at my house, the mother started laughing and said, "Why don't you pray for him?"

I asked if I could lay hands on him, and when I started praying, the Spirit of the Lord fell on him, and he looked like he was stunned. There was definitely a holy hush in the room. Later, when the sheik got home, he told Suleiman, "Some Christians must really love God."

Thank you, Lord, for letting your power be a witness to whom we are in you!

Blake Leaves for London

Blake in London

One day, in the summer of 2004, Blake said, "I cannot take it anymore. There are refugees in our house every day. They do not bathe, and they steal from us. Mom, I love the people, but I do not feel I am supposed to live with them in the refugee camp. I want to go back to London."

He was around sixteen at that time, and I did not want him to go. Suleiman said that everyone in the refugee camp would think I was a bad mother if I let my son go at such a young age.

I prayed about it, and God said, "Give him to me and just watch what I will do."

It was one of the hardest decisions of my life, but I knew I could not hold him prisoner. I knew in my heart that my son and I should be working together for the Lord, but forcing him to stay would be worse than him leaving.

Blake would send me e-mails from London and call to tell me about life on his own. He was starving most of the time. He lived with his girlfriend. At dinnertime, he would try to eat with his girlfriend's family. The boyfriend of the girl's mother, who was either stoned or drunk, would often beat Blake up and did not allow him to eat. I longed for him to come back, but Blake did not want to return to Jericho. He felt his life in London was better than living in the Palestinian refugee camp.

On my birthday, Blake sent me a ceramic hand with a candle in it from London. My heart was broken that he would take the small amount of funds he had and mail me such a thoughtful gift. Blake e-mailed me and said, "Mom, I knew you would know that this was the hand of God."

I surely did and cried at the e-mail and at the goodness of the Lord.

Later, when the house fires came, the cross on the wall and the ceramic hand from Blake remained intact. Even though they are both damaged from the fires, I have kept them to this day.

Blake is an excellent video editor, and after about a year and a half of hard times for him in London, a company hired him for high wages of eighteen pounds per hour. He told me later that he was making more money than he knew how to manage and said he never wanted to return to Jericho.

I had many prophecies about my son working with me, that he would be a great one upon the earth. When he is not at Living Bread, I feel such a void in the atmosphere. God had told me to let him go and that he would take care of him. I kept my trust in the Lord and knew it was the only way.

Blake had left two close Palestinian friends behind, Suleiman and Mohammad. When Blake left for London, those two young boys told him they were going to watch over me like I was their own mother. Every day, they would come to the refugee camp to see if I was doing okay. I was amazed at their loyalty. This would cost them two shekels every day for a taxi, and yet they never missed day. They made a promise to my son and were faithful to it. People used to go to the mosque and threaten Suleiman's father because his son was hanging around me. The harassment got so bad that Suleiman's father said I could not visit his family home anymore. However, Suleiman continued his daily visits to my house.

Mohammad Encounters Jesus Christ

Mohammad's Vision

I loved to pray with Suleiman and Mohammad. One day, they told me they were going to have their own prayer meeting after they left that night. They said they were going to stay up most of the night and pray. I was surprised. I was awakened at two o'clock in the morning by a call from Mohammad. He said Jesus came, and that they could not tell me on the phone what happened but that they would tell me about it in the morning.

When they arrived the next morning, I could hardly wait to hear the story. They said they shut all the lights off and waited for the Lord. I am not sure why they decided to have the lights all off. Suleiman said that when the Lord came, all he could see was a light on Mohammad.

Jesus took Mohammad's hand and said, "Mohammad, follow me."

Mohammad told us that he looked into the eyes of the Lord and began to melt. He told us that when the Lord took his hand, he felt like there was a fire burning all over him. Mohammad said it was so extreme that it was nearly unbearable. I knew in the Spirit that the Lord was calling for all those that follow Mohammad the prophet to follow him.

Another night, the Lord came to Mohammad in a dream and showed him an amazing thing. He told him a story about a preacher who was asking the Lord for truth. The preacher went up a mountain and met a bird. The bird gave him a message. Mohammad took a piece of paper and cut it up like he saw the Lord do in a vision and laid it on a table for us. In Arabic, it said hell, and as he opened the last piece of paper, it was a cross. Mohammad said as he held up the cross, "God saved you from hell by the cross."

Breaking into a Fasted Lifestyle

Jericho had a small outbreak of the swine flu. The rumor in the refugee camp was that Israel was buying all the chickens in the West Bank because they thought that Palestinians did not know how to handle the problem properly. The refugees were finding dead chickens. Even though the people were starving, they would kill and bury all the chickens in the yard because of the swine flu.

I met a taxi driver who said he had jaundice and hepatitis B from the local meat. We heard that others were also sick. The Lord told us to go on a Daniel fast, which has been modified nine years later into a kosher dairy diet. This is the promise God gave to Daniel:

> So the overseer continued to withhold their choice food and the wine they were to drink, and kept giving them vegetables. As for these four youths, God gave them knowledge and intelligence in every branch of literature and wisdom; Daniel even understood all kinds of visions and dreams.
>
> Daniel 1:16–17 (NASB)

We knew God wanted us to fast so he could teach us and bless us. The Lord also showed us that by living a fasted lifestyle, we would be ready and able to cast out demons with the word. This is our call. We are so blessed to be a part of his divine plan.

Refugee Camp Testimonies

Palestinian Refugees outreach to the poor

People were hungry in the refugee camps, and their cupboards were bare. We went to homes where we knew the children did not have any bread to eat. The children hungrily eyed the bag of bread or box of juice we brought for them to eat and drink. I had never seen people as hungry as I did in Jericho. The medical need was also very great. Every family seemed to have someone that needed some kind of surgery. We made a corporate medical policy that we provided no medical aid. We would offer healing through Jesus Christ.

We knew that Jesus Christ would heal the people. We felt this would be a great testimony in these people's lives. The Lord was faithful, and his love touched the multitude. Deaf ears opened, the mute spoke, and the lame walked. When Jesus Christ went to the cross, he conquered death, hell, and sickness. His blood is the reconciliation that brings us spotless before the Father. The work of the cross and the blood of the Lamb is the doorway to eternity.

The refugees were still coming to the house every day. We decided to have a church meeting with them each week and teach them the Bible. We would meet and talk about Jesus and then give them bags of rice. We would pray for the sick and comfort those in mourning. God did miracles! One man walked in the house and said, "I can hear for the first time in years." He said he wanted to go home and see if he could hear inside of his own house. We had not had a chance to pray for that man, the anointing just fell on him when he entered the house. God is great and works his own agenda!

Three men from Aqabat Jaber refugee camp began to visit me in the Ein as-Sultan refugee camp where I lived. We would sit down together in my living room, and I would pray for them. They would visit me for a couple hours, and after they left, they would discuss things about the visit. One day, something happened to them. They said, "Did you feel that?" Apparently, all three of them felt running water flowing over their feet as I prayed for them. I did not know about this until later, but their mission had been to destroy me.

After those prayer times together, the men were changed. One had prostate cancer; God answered our prayers, and he was healed. Another man said, "I have a nine-year-old daughter, and the Koran says that Mohammad had a nine-year-old wife. When I look at my daughter, I am concerned about this, and I think this is wrong." He stated that he would like to learn about Christianity.

In time, all three men opened up their hearts to me. They said, "For us to think about Christianity is difficult because we see our children learning Islam every day at school." They said if they spoke to their children about Christianity, they would tell their friends at school, and it could mean death or persecution for the entire family. Those are some very hard decisions to make in an all-Muslim community, but the Lord gives a greater grace. You can never do more for God than he can do for you.

Jericho was a sealed off city. No one was coming in, and no one was going out. Some Messianic Jews from northern Israel contacted me and said it was on their hearts to do something for the Palestinians. They wanted to bring in a truck full of supplies.

They were afraid to come to the checkpoint, so I was supposed to meet them at the gas station at Almog Junction, just outside the city. As they were handing over all the supplies, they began to weep. They said, "Please tell the Palestinians that we love them." They gave me a lot of baby blankets. I took them into the refugee camp and began handing them out. I had the translator who was with me tell the Palestinians that these were gifts from the Israelis. I shared with them how the Israelis said they loved them. The Palestinians had tears flowing as I passed out baby blankets. They were so moved that the Israelis cared for their children.

I also decided to take some of gifts to newborns in the hospital. We made up packages with Bibles, baby blankets, and baby supplies and took them to the Jericho hospital. I hoped that the barriers dividing these two peoples could become a bridge with the love of God. In Genesis 25:9, it says Ishmael and Jacob buried Abraham together in Hebron. They came together in death. Surely, the Author of Life could bring these brothers together again.

Love Breaks Through

Jericho refugee camp

Karen Dunham with refugee children in the camp

A small group of friends from Jerusalem brought used clothes to Jericho. The refugees loved them. They were receiving them as if they were very special.

At that time, I was also wearing donated clothes, washing them in buckets of water, and I had not had a haircut for nearly two years. I had been taking cold showers and was thinking I would be in the refugee camp forever. During those times, in my walk with the Lord, some of the dreams he had given me about the future seemed a long way off. Taking care of the broken people who were in front of me was what he wanted me to do.

We had our weekly service in the refugee camp. I was in tune with the Spirit after spending days with God, and I looked forward to the weekly camp meetings. A really special move of the Spirit happened at one of these meetings. I asked all the refugees if they would be quiet for a few minutes because I wanted to make a promotional DVD to send to America. I was speaking in English the following message:

> God heard the boy crying, and the Angel of God called to Hagar from heaven and said to her, "What is the matter, Hagar? Do not be afraid; God has heard the boy crying as he lies there. Lift the boy up and take him by the hand, for I will make him into a great nation." Then God opened her eyes and she saw a well of water. So she went and filled the skin with water and gave the boy a drink.
>
> Genesis 21:17–19 (NIV)

I asked the people who would be watching the DVD to hold up the hands of the Palestinian children like Hagar did with Ishmael. God promised in his word he would make Ishmael a great nation. We all know there is nothing great without God in the center of it. All of a sudden, the Arabs who were gathered in the camp were responding, jumping up and down, and cheering. I had to get a translator to come up to the front.

I asked the translator, "Why are they making all this noise? We asked them to be quiet."

The translator said, "They heard the message and understood it and said it was a very good message."

I was amazed at the power of God. Most of them spoke Arabic, yet they heard the message as I spoke in English and rejoiced over it.

Later, I asked God what happened. He said, "The language of love will always break through." He said, "Tell my people to go to the nations with the language of love, and it will not fail." People understand the message of love, and the walls will fall.

Call to Media

Blake Davis

A man called Pastor Decker called me one day and invited me to come to Jerusalem to meet someone from the media. At the time of the call, I had nothing to wear to the meeting. I looked at the pile of clothes in the living room that the refugees had been going through and spotted a beautiful designer suit made from silk. I praised God for people who throw away designer suits and laughed as I found it to be a perfect fit. God is our source, and he is right on time for everything.

I arrived at the Dan Pearl Hotel in Jerusalem and met the senior programmer for LeSEA Broadcasting. After being in the refugee camp for so long, I was amazed by the splendor of the hotel. During the conversation with David, the programmer, he said that he wanted to help me feed the poor. Then he asked, "How fast can you make an international television show?"

As I heard those words, I felt my whole spirit jumping inside me. Mountains began to fall. I knew everything in my life had brought me to this moment. That was the destiny that God had inside of me all along. The King was taking us on the airwaves. I had such a powerful witness to what he said that I almost shook. I had a quickening from God that I was exactly where I was supposed to be at that moment. I answered, "Sure, in a few months."

At that time, I had no idea what breaking into media was all about. I was driven by the passion to know Christ and the destiny he had for me. I want you to know, you may be in a prison or you may be in a pit, but destiny will hunt you down and find you. Maybe you are flipping burgers for a season, but the promise of God and word of the Lord will hunt you down. Destiny is coming for you just as he promised. Expect him to find you where you are.

Catching the Vision

Teaching the Word of God

One day, during my quiet time with the Lord, I saw this magnificent, beautiful desert with golden sand and no water. In the vision, the desert was covered with mallard ducks. Many ducks were walking across the desert with no water. The Lord told me, "The Palestinian people are going to be like those ducks. When you hand them the word of God, it is going to be just like taking those ducks to water. They are going to know how to swim, and they are going to love the word of God." This was such an encouraging word from God. Assuredly, that vision is already coming to pass.

I was praying on the phone with Abraham, a friend of mine, who had given his life to Jesus. He was very sick, and I began to pray for him. Becoming very excited, he shouted, "I can feel it all over me. It is coming through the phone!"

I laughed and said, "It is not coming through the phone. It is coming from heaven."

He said, "You have to come over right away."

I came over with a Bible and gave it to him. Five days later, his eyes were shining when he said, "I read the whole thing. I just could not stop. As I read it, I felt my blood rushing and the hairs standing up on my arm." Abraham added, "I am going to read it again."

I told him, "That is a great idea." I laughed to myself.

It is so amazing to bring the word of God to a people who have never read it or heard it taught. I realized that not many of the Palestinians are educated in the Bible, yet they claim to believe in it. It is God's mercy to give a full Bible to every Arab.

Many Arabs have no idea where Israel came from, nor her authority. It is not taught to children in the schools. The Bible is Israel's proof of having a right to exist and shows the heart of God for all people. No one is left out of his glorious promises through his son, Jesus Christ.

While we were still living in the refugee camp, I felt the Lord tell me to drive a stake. I hung a sign outside the house that said, "Living Bread International Church." I knew it was about souls, not a sign, but God wanted me to do it. People from all over the refugee camp came and just stared at the sign. I asked Mahmood, a neighbor, why everyone was looking at it. He said that they felt something good when they looked at the sign. Twenty-four hours later, the sign went missing. The landlady had the stolen sign on her roof, so we did not put another sign up in that house.

One night, a general of Palestinian president Arafat called me up and said, "Jesus is in my house. What should I do?"

I told him, "How can you say no to Jesus? Do whatever he asks you to do."

The man confessed he had a problem with women. I told him he should talk to Jesus about it because he would wash him in his blood and give him a clean conscience. At that time, I wondered, *When Jesus Christ comes in a vision or a dream, how can anyone ever say no to the King?*

The word about Living Bread International Church in Jericho began to spread. A loving couple named Jan and Gregory heard about us and started bringing teams from all over the world to Jericho. They brought people to lead worship from Rick Riding's prayer house. Rick was very happy for him and his people to be sowing into a move of God in Jericho. I was amazed myself as the church began to grow and grow. The death threats also grew, and people continued to harass us. Some even said it was illegal for us to live in the Islamic refugee camp. But no matter what happened, the devil could not steal our peace.

> For the mountains shall depart and the hills be removed, but my kindness shall not depart from you, nor shall my covenant of peace be removed," says the LORD, who has mercy on you.
>
> Isaiah 54:10 (NKJV)

I discovered that Christian refugees were not allowed to live in the Palestinian refugee camps because the camps were Islamic. The governor of the city had said that I had to stop evangelizing, or they were going to force me to leave the city. It was only by the grace of God that we were able to remain in Jericho. Eventually, the governor of the city said, "We do not think that giving away Bibles is evangelism, so you can give them to anyone you want to." Working for the Lord is fantastic and exciting; I never wanted to stop.

Regularly, people used to show up at my door with dreams and visions. One morning, we had prayed for the romance of the Lord to be released in the camp. We wanted Jesus to show them how much he loved them. Later in the day, a woman came and brought her friend along to translate. She said, "I had a dream with Jesus. Jesus kissed me on the cheek." I asked her what she said to Jesus Christ. Lowering her eyes, she softly answered, "I told him that was not proper in my culture." That was the first fruit of our prayers.

Refugee camp life was rough, and I had no experience living in such conditions. There was a problem with scorpions, and we often went without water. People were always at the door. They came because they needed food or medical treatment. It was very hot outside, and there was no water in the camp. The word in the camp at that time was that the Israeli army had stolen all the water. People were hungry, hot, and very angry.

I knew the Israeli army was not stealing the water. I went to the water municipality to find out what was happening. The municipality in Jericho said, "They are not paying their bills in the refugee camp."

I said, "I do pay my bills."

They replied, "When one suffers, you all suffer."

It was the heat of summer, terrorist activities were very high, and now the poorest of the poor were suffering at the hands of their own Palestinian government. There was no air-conditioning, and we were going without water in the lowest and one of the hottest places on earth. We all had swamp coolers to cool the air, but at times, it was so hot that I cried. Many afternoons, we lay in our rooms and could not move because of the heat.

The Rich Young Ruler

After one year in Ein as-Sultan refugee camp, we moved to Elisha's Spring. We rented a six-bedroom house with a garage on the bottom floor. The Lord told us to fast from the world's social cup of coffee and tea. I saw a globe with black liquid pouring down over it and spilling all over the globe. I asked the Lord what it was, and he said it was coffee and tea—the world's largest household god. The Lord said we were to fast from coffee and tea and that his word would cover the globe as I had seen the liquid flow over the earth. We were already living a fasted lifestyle. The Lord told me the blessing that I was a part of was the same magnitude of coffee and tea reaching the ends of the earth. God gives seed to them who will sow. Coffee and tea had just become our God seed. People from all around the world who were volunteering with our ministry would ask, "What about decaffeinated coffee or herbal tea?" Missionary teams would say, "If we cannot have our coffee, we are not coming."

I never realized until that time how numerous the chains that hold people in bondage were. They would call me names and say I did not hear from God, but I kept going. I knew his voice. It was the same voice that had pulled me out of hell, and I was going to obey no matter what. Even when it hurt me and my reputation or caused the volunteers to leave, I was determined to obey.

Through one of my real estate transactions in 1995, I had purchased a gas station and kept it in trust for my son. It was a bank foreclosure, but they were afraid of taking title to it because of previous tank leaks, so they sold it to me at a great price. After I bought it, I rented it out. I still had the gas station when I lived in Jericho. The monthly rent I received helped take care of Blake and me and also feed some of the poor people. That income supported us in the mission field since we had no supporters at that time. We received a thousand dollars per month for a few years and then it increased to fifteen hundred dollars per month until we sold it. It was now the spring of 2004. The Lord taught me about the rich young ruler.

> When Jesus heard this, he said to him, "One thing you still lack; sell all that you possess and distribute it to the poor, and you shall have treasure in heaven; and come, follow me."
>
> Luke 18:22 (NASB)

And the Lord said to me:

"You still lack one thing. Sell all you have and distribute it to the poor, and you will have treasure in heaven."

The people in the refugee camps were starving, and the Lord was telling me I was still a rich young ruler. The Lord spoke to me and said, "I want to bless those people."

I asked, "You want to bless these people? How do you want to bless them?"

The Lord said, "I want you to go home and sell your gas station and give the proceeds to them."

I wondered if I was hearing correctly. I went over the scripture again and kept seeing the word *lack*. Finally, I looked it up in the Strong's Concordance. The word *lack* means to "not finish the race." So the rich young ruler was asking the Lord, "What will it take for me to finish the race?" The Lord said, "Give everything to the poor and follow me."

I meditated on what it meant to follow God and give up everything. God was giving me the same invitation as he did the rich young ruler. No matter what I did, I did not want to be disqualified because of one thing lacking. More than anything else, I wanted to finish well.

When we arrived in the United States, I told Blake how the Lord wanted me to sell the gas station and give the money to the poor. He knew the gas station was in trust for him as an inheritance when he got older. He said, "I am going to have to go to work."

I told Blake, "Even though you do not understand it, the Lord is going to bountifully bless you. It is not just about giving to the poor. It is a heavenly investment for you son. God is surely going to bless you."

When we sold it, we took $150 thousand as a down payment, with a balance of $100 thousand due. I gave the purchaser a five-year mortgage.

When the money stopped coming in, God, the best public relations manager in the world, touched enough hearts, and we started getting international support. They heard about our tribulations and wanted to help.

Elisha's Spring

Elisha Spring

Burnt out house

When we moved into the first house close to the Elisha's Spring, we had a lot of trouble with our neighbors. We used to give away food donations from the garage of the house. The landlord's nephew, who worked for the jail, wanted us to leave. He was embarrassed that his family had rented the house to Christians.

One night, they placed a stack of tires against the doorway and around the front of the building and then set the tires on fire. The heat of the fire blew the glass out of the entrance door. Black smoke from the tires flooded the house on both floors, and our wiring box burnt up. We called the police, but they did not come. We realized our water had been cut off. Finally, we went up to the top of the roof and made a phone call to the liaison officer on the Israeli side. We asked him to try to convince the Palestinians to send a fire truck. Eventually, the fire simply went out by itself. The interior of the cement house was charred black.

A man named Samir came over to wash the walls with bleach. He wanted to work day and night, cleaning and painting the house to help us. The whole time we were praying, blessing, and honoring the Lord, thanking him that everyone was all right.

Later, Samir asked if he could go home for a couple of hours. I had a volunteer working with me named Thomas. Thomas was such a Godly man, and he had the heart to see the Spirit move among the people.

When Samir came back, we asked him, "What did you do? Why did you go home?"

He amazed us with his matter-of-fact reply, "I went home and told my whole family about Jesus. They all have Jesus in their hearts now."

Thomas and I started crying. Thomas said, "If this is what it takes for them to receive Jesus in their hearts, then send the fires, God!"

A small group of policemen appeared the next day. As they were leaving, each asked if they might receive a Bible. I thought to myself, *We think they broke in, but really the fire of God broke out!*

Another woman came to visit from the refugee camp. As soon as we laid hands on her, demons flew out of her. She was wailing as the Lord delivered her from years of depression. Later, when her husband was gone, she invited us over to her house. She had two teenage daughters who were not allowed to read, write, or leave their house, which was small and dirty. They hated their father and would hide books around the house. The girls treasured their hidden books. I tried to give them a gospel tract and a Bible, but the woman was terrified of her husband.

I remember wondering how it could be legal to oppress those girls. They told me that in the refugee camps, many of the women are not allowed to study past the sixth grade in school. I think this is to keep them from believing they can have anything better than a life of servitude. We have so much to pray for as we serve a God who answers prayer.

Worship and Miracles

Little girl that began to walk

By the time spring arrived, I was still living in the house by
Elisha's Spring. I received a visit from my American friends, Lila
Terhune and Karen Goodman. They told me, "If you will bring
worship into your house, God will make things a lot easier for
you." We immediately started a daily worship watch in the house.
We felt there was a special blessing for getting up early in the

morning. We started having early morning watches, though it was very hard on my young volunteers. Miracles were breaking out, and with worship, everything was so much greater. Along with the intercessors that prayed us through the storms, worship was the abundant oil that kept the wheels turning.

I went into an electrical store one day, and there stood three men dressed in white robes. They blocked the doorway and would not allow anyone to enter. They looked like the religious Islamic society. I thought to myself, *What is going on?*

I felt like the Spirit of the Lord said, "You are blessed in the city."

A man came over toward me and sat down in a chair. He and the other man spoke to me in English. He said, "We heard the power of God is with you. You must pray for this man." As I prayed for him, the power of God came upon him, and he was immediately healed. Although we could not understand his Arabic, it seemed that he had been suffering from severe pain in his knees, which made it difficult for him to walk. They were all laughing, and I was allowed to leave. I was amazed at what the Lord had done and very pleased to learn that I had a reputation of one that carries God's power.

A few days later, a Bedouin man, who spent most of his time in the mountains with his goats, came up to the house. He told Eyad and Ahmed, my translators and future pastors, that he wanted me to baptize him. I asked them, "What does he know about Jesus and baptism?"

They told me he had visions about Jesus and that Jesus said I should baptize him. I told him to return on Friday for a teaching video.

When he came back on Friday, I played a video of Jesus from the gospel of Luke for him. Then I told Eyad that if the man wanted to be baptized after watching the movie, I would gladly baptize him. He sat in the living room and cried the whole time the video was playing. When he finished watching the video, I baptized him. Then the man returned to the mountains. This man could not read or write. His full discipleship was what he could see and hear. The Spirit of God was surely teaching and speaking to this Bedouin who wandered into our place that day. The Palestinians know that no one had the power to change a heart but God.

Mohammad, one of our church members, came to me and said, "Please go to the hospital and pray for my mother." She was the mother of two teenage daughters who were prisoners in their house. She was in critical condition in the Jericho hospital, so I went to visit her. She shared her hospital room with two other sick women. As I prayed for her, the power of God filled the room. The other ladies motioned me over to their beds. I prayed over them and laid hands on all three of them. When I left the hospital I thought, *Wow, God! It is so amazing to pray for all these Muslim women and see them being healed by your power in the name of Jesus Christ.*

The next day, Mohammad came over to me and said, "I picked my mother up from the hospital today. She told me that all the women you had prayed for in her room were healed." Books could never record all that God does when you flow with the rhythm of his Spirit. God is amazing.

There was a woman who brought her crippled granddaughter to our church each week. Whenever large groups and teams came to town, I would ask them to pray for the little girl. For months, people laid hands on this girl and prayed for her. She was four years old and had never walked. Her legs were completely bowed. Then one night, we were getting ready to have a meeting when the grandmother walked in and said, "Would you take a picture of the girl for her mother?" She then told me that the girl's mother had abandoned her long ago because of her inability to walk. She also said, "I want to get a picture of her because this morning, she got up and started walking!"

One day, a local taxi driver brought three men over to my house. He said, "These three men asked to speak to someone about Jesus." They were all asking questions, and I told them about the kingdom of God.

They asked me, "How do you pray? How do you hold your hands? Do you open your eyes?" They were trying to see how I sat. They tried to hold their hands the same way I held mine. I was amused and explained to them, "It is not about any of these things. It is about knowing Jesus personally."

When I spoke to the man who wore a white gown and cap, he said, "What about me? Is there room for me in this kingdom that you speak? Is there room for my two wives and my twenty children?" Immediately, the Spirit hit me, and I heard from the Father, "They do not know they are welcome. Tell them they are all welcome, and they can come into my kingdom as they are." All are welcome in the kingdom of God. Their families, their wives, and their children are all welcome. Jesus paid the price for them all at Calvary, and his kingdom and his arms are open; for whosoever calls upon the name of Jesus Christ will be saved. I am so glad God gave me this revelation because it came up often. The God I serve loves everyone, and all are welcome in his kingdom.

Eyad, one of my translators and a future pastor, came to me one day and said, "I need to go to Jordan to find a woman who loves Jesus more than my wife, because she does not love Jesus as much as I do."

I replied, "No, you cannot go and get another wife just because your wife does not love Jesus. You are not allowed to have a second wife. You come as you are. If you came to Jesus with two wives, then you take care of both of them and your children. You, however, came to Jesus with one wife, and so that is what you are to have."

By that point, our outreaches looked like a branch of the UN. We had to use bodyguards because people were pushing and shoving in the garage where food was distributed. We would individually package rice in small bags and place several packages in a huge burlap rice bag. Then we had our bodyguards take these huge burlap rice bags. They had to run to the street as fast as they could. The people would go wild because they were so hungry. There was no standing in line or any other form of order. They would punch, hit, and fight for the rice. The bags would break, and rice would spill out all over the place.

One night, a woman asked me if she could help clean up the place after the food giveaway. She swept up all the spilled rice on the floor of the garage and on the street. When she finished, there were piles of dirt and rice mixed together. She asked, "Can I have this pile?" My heart broke for that woman in her desperation. Seeing her sweep up garbage mixed with rice and then ask me for it touched me deeply. It was nothing but garbage to us. We rejoiced as we gave her all that we had left on our shelves and a one fifty-pound bag of flour that the crowds overlooked.

The church continuously administered aid and the good news of the gospel. The militant neighbors threatened us, and it seemed like we were in spiritual warfare all the time. The secular men would tell us that groups of Hamas men were coming for us. Our Palestinian employees would go to the head sheikh and ask if they were planning to try and kill us. Repeatedly, we would get a message back that all is well. Then at night, fires would come. But no matter what, we were not leaving.

Fires

Jericho officers after a Molotov fire incident

Molotov cocktail

Burnt out car

The ministry at our Elisha's Spring house was rapidly expanding and so was the wickedness in heavenly places. They were now playing a more deadly game. A Molotov cocktail was thrown through our volunteer Thomas's bedroom window, causing his mattress to light up in flames. After that incident, my volunteers were concerned about sleeping on the second floor, since it seemed to be a target area for the gas bombs. I moved the volunteers up to the top floor, and I moved myself down to the middle floor. The team purchased a rope, painted it red, and tied it to our roof.

We called it our Rahab rope, after the story of Rahab in the book of Joshua. We thought if the fires became too hot, we could slide down the rope to safety. More than once, the fires below kept us stranded on the roof. One night, the building was on fire again from another Molotov cocktail. This was probably our third fire at this house.

I called the Israeli army and asked them to please call the fire department because the water had been turned off. They asked, "What are you doing?"

I said, "We are standing at the wall."

The soldier asked, "What do you mean? What is that noise?"

I explained to him that it was music, and we were worshipping the Lord, like he did at the Western Wall. When the enemy is trying to take you out, one of the greatest victories you can have is to worship God. Bless him in the low places and watch him elevate you out of trouble. The soldier said, "I cannot wait to meet you."

The landlord was practically crying for us to leave because of his nephew's grumbling. The nephew's friends threw fire at us and harassed our volunteers with life-threatening words. We were constantly under pressure to move out of the house by Elisha's Spring. Today, we have a house the Lord has given us right on Elisha's Springs, which is where the school of prophets still hangs out.

Back to the Refugee Camp

Car fire

Refugee camp

The deputy mayor of Jericho told Isaac, our helper there, that his friend had a house for rent that was the most secure house in the land. He told him that the house was located in a good neighborhood, and he was sure that I would love it. I had no idea where the house was located, but I felt in my heart that I would surely like it. The owner of the house was one of President Arafat's top security officers.

As I was being driven out to see the house, I nearly fainted when the driver turned back into the refugee camp. I thought, "Really, God, you are moving me back into the refugee camp?"

Blake was visiting again from London. He loved the people of Jericho, but not the refugee camp lifestyle. I appreciated my son periodically coming back to help me. Blake was very talented in video, and people were always amazed at his work. I told God, "If Blake tells me I should move back into the refugee camp, then I will know it is of you." This was a huge fleece.

I asked Blake to take a look at the house with me. When I arrived at the house, I asked him if I should move there. Blake said, "Mom, you came for the people, so you should live with the people." I was very amused and seemed to have heart flutters, but I knew he was right. We moved back into the refugee camp.

This was our third house, and we were determined to have the best security. We had metal bars, screens, and shields installed over the windows. With the windows secured, a Molotov bomb would just bounce off. People used to say it looked more like an army barrack than a ministry house. We started having weekly meetings at the house and had one hundred to one hundred forty people attending some of our meetings. We also received frequent death threats and warnings.

Jordan River

Gateway to Jordan River at Jericho

Officers at Jordan River

Back then, you had to get special permission to go to the Jordan River, which was under military patrol. The liaison officers used to notify me when the Catholics or Orthodox Christians were going to be at the Jordan River, granting my team and me permission to go too. I loved the Jordan River and felt it was one of the most important places in Israel. One time, an officer asked if I enjoyed going to the river with Catholic and Orthodox groups. I said, "Yes, they are Christians but not like the Evangelical people."

He replied, "Maybe we could get you your own day at the river."

At the same time that the Israeli army was giving us permission for an annual day at the Jordan River, prophets around the world were declaring that the bride of Christ was crossing over the Jordan River. People would send me the articles. I knew it was important to worship in the Spirit at the Jordan River, in the doorway to the land where Joshua brought all of Israel across on dry ground.

That is also where Jesus Christ was baptized and where the voice of the Father came through the open heavens and declared, "This is my Son in whom I am well pleased." That is where the Spirit of the Lord came upon Jesus Christ in bodily form. That doorway is also where Elisha crossed over the river with a double portion of the Spirit on his way to heal the waters in the city of Jericho, known as Elisha's Springs. That is where John the Baptist ministered to prepare the way of the Lord. That is where the ax head floated, the man with leprosy was healed, and where King David crossed over. That chief doorway is where Israel left the wilderness and crossed into the promised land, and we worship in that place often.

On January 11, we held an event at the doorway to the land—the Jordan River. At that time, there was a steep path down to the river. We took our Palestinian congregation with us, and the church members were playing the drums, singing, and waving banners. One of the liaison officers came and said his boss wanted to see me.

The man asked me, "Why do they look like Muslims but act like Christians?"

I answered him, saying, "It has nothing to do with what they wear, but everything to do with their hearts. With God, it is always about the heart, not the clothes."

I met with an official from the Israeli Ministry of Tourism through my friend Vicki Hodd, who is also a tourist agent in Israel. She had arranged a meeting at the river with the Israeli army, the Ministry of Tourism, and the defense attorney for the minister's office. Vicki instructed me to bring all the scriptural references I had regarding the Jordan River.

After the big meeting at the Jordan River, one of them asked me to pray for them. It was a surreal moment for me as I prayed blessings over the Jewish people at the Jordan River. After that, the Israeli government released $20 million to build a site for visitors at that spot on the Jordan River. Today, the site is open daily, and it is fantastic to be a small grain of sand in this eternal testimony.

> They will rebuild the ancient ruins and restore the places long devastated; they will renew the ruined cities that have been devastated for generations.
>
> Isaiah 61:4 (NIV)

Coming through
the Eastern Gateway

I crossed over to Jordan and spent a few days there with part of my team. When we arrived back at the Jordanian border crossing to return to Israel, we found it was completely closed. We did not want to stay another night in Jordan, so I asked the officers who was allowed to cross the border. They replied, "Only diplomats." The Jordanian officers told us the only way they would let us cross over the Allenby Bridge was if an Israeli officer called them and gave them permission. I phoned Barak, the liaison officer in Jericho. I had no idea at the time how lofty a request that was, but it worked.

It took about an hour and a half for someone to escort us through the many checkpoints. We felt so important and thankful. I felt like God had entered the eastern gateway and had carried us across, through the doorway into the good land. It was an ordeal on the Israeli side as well because they also had many checkpoints. At that time, I knew something significant had happened and that it was huge in the Spirit. I understood we had traveled the pathway of the King through the eastern gateway into the promised land.

Pleading for Help

During that time, Christians from around the world began coming to visit me in Jericho. They told me the refugees were starving because I was not asking for help from the larger ministries in Jerusalem. They gave me a list of names and told me I needed to let them know the condition of the refugees and that if another refugee went without food, it would be my fault. Under conviction, many people had looked at the big problem rather than helping feed the one in front of them. They believed that if the larger ministries only knew the hardships of the people in Jericho, they would grant immediate aid. The job was massive, and they just kept telling us to go to Jerusalem and plead for help.

I made appointments with the largest organizations I could find. The first organization I approached told me they could not help because Jericho was a terrorist zone and sending aid would affect the official status of the organization. I felt the next organization was worried about their reputation. I realized I was wasting God's time because none of these people had any conviction to help the Palestinians.

In my last meeting with one of the embassy leaders, I recounted our recent trip over the Jordan River. I told him about being able to cross from Jordan to Israel through all those checkpoints and how we were treated like royalty. As I was explaining how the Israeli army had shown us tremendous favor and had arranged with the Jordanian military for the gate to be opened so we could cross the border, a powerful anointing fell upon us. It was like sheets of intense rain as God invaded the meeting. The man standing there with me stood up and said, "God has given you the keys to unlock the door for Israel. He has placed a jewel in your hand. Do not lose it!" The fire of God was so heavy on both of us that tears were streaming from my eyes. All this running around and pleading for the poor had brought me to this place. The weight of the prophetic blessing that had been spoken left me speechless. I went back to Jericho without any aid, but I had a word from God that would carry me into the next season. Then the Lord spoke to me, "Do not run after anything. Let me bring it to your feet."

I agreed, "Yes, Lord."

About a year later, the Christian Friends of Israel found our ministry and sent us large quantities of clothing for the refugees. The refugees would sometimes have tears coming down their cheeks as we handed out the deluge of blessings that came from this organization. We will never forget the courageous and loving leadership of Sharon Sanders from Christian Friends of Israel.

Media Breakthrough

Blake Davis and Karen Dunham

God told me he wanted to go through the 10/40 Window. The 10/40 Window, an area between 10° and 40° north latitude, is considered the most unreachable part of the world for the gospel. The networks were telling me, "Do not be foolish. You have to go raise money in America first and then go buy broadcast time in the 10/40 Window." But God clearly told us it was his garden, and he wanted us to broadcast through there.

At that time, we did not have much money at all, but we had a contract with LeSEA Broadcasting. Jan and Gregory Kuske had given us a donation to start broadcasting, so we were able to pay the first two months. More than the money, we appreciated the great encouragement and love we felt from those two. God told us to sign the contract for one year, and we did.

Since that day, the Lord has always been there to cover the broadcasting costs. Before we began airing, we asked a high-ranking officer to watch twelve of the shows. After watching the shows, he said, "I would suggest you run as fast as you can with this." We had a green light to air in Israel and sent the shows to the network. Those at the network prayed about it, and the manager said, "We are on the air." Of course, today, the internet is the way to reach people you would never dream you could reach.

Reconciliation

Isaac, Eyad, and Thomas Franks in Ein As Sultan

During that time, I was holding discipleship classes with my two interpreters, Eyad and Ahmed. I was teaching them on the subject of forgiveness. Eyad said he could not go any further with Jesus. "I just cannot forgive my father for leaving my mother and going to Gaza."

Later on in the meeting, Ahmed said, "English I know, Arabic I know, but what is this?" He started speaking in tongues. The Spirit of the Lord never ceased to amaze me. After this wonderful invasion of the Spirit, I said to Eyad, "Let's ask Jesus Christ for the power to forgive your father."

The next day, Eyad told me he had called his father in Gaza. I asked him what happened. He traced lines down his face with his hands, showing tears, and then he said he hung up the phone. I told Eyad what an outstanding job he had done and how proud the Lord was of him. I continued, "Jesus will give you more power to forgive, and one day, you will be able to speak with your father."

A couple of days later, Eyad's sister called him. She told him that she saw a missed call from him to their father. He told his sister that he was crying too hard to speak to his father. Then Eyad and his father spoke to each other and in tears, the two were on the phone together for an hour.

A few years later, we took a video of Eyad to Gaza with us. We also brought Eyad a video of his father in Gaza, who had not seen him in years, and they became fully reconciled. Not long after that, Eyad's father died. God was so good to have given them reconciliation before his father's passing.

Eyad continued to grow in the Lord. He told us the Lord was telling him he would be going to Iran and Iraq to share the gospel of Jesus. He said Jesus had told him he was going to die for him one day. Then he asked me, "Is the church going to take care of my children when I die?" Right then, a sword hit my heart. I know that in Islam, when a person is a martyr for Mohammad, their families are supported, but what does the Christian church do for a martyr's families?

The Palestinians are baby lions when they meet Jesus Christ. They want to take on the entire world for him. I find it an honor to be with these people in missions to reach the poor, pray for the needy, and educate the illiterate with the good news of the gospel.

More Fires and Tribulation

Burnt out car

Thomas Franks in Ein As-Sultan refugee camp

Back in the refugee camp, the neighbors would sit out on their rooftops, watching us as we anointed the Palestinian congregation. We were teaching the Bible, praying for the sick, and singing and dancing with the people. The neighbors would watch and wait on their rooftops until the middle of the night. Then they would start throwing Molotov cocktails through the windows of the house and at the cars. I lost count of the number of mattresses burned by Molotov cocktails. Cleaning the soot off the walls and repainting the house had become part of our regular duties.

On church day at the house, neighbors would throw stones at the women and children who were trying to come down the road to church. Mothers would hide their babies in their shirts as they tried to make it safely down the street. We had our own guards in the streets to protect those who were trying to come. I was always amazed and proud of the Palestinians that would break through and come, despite the danger. Even as they were being threatened, called names, and stoned, they could not be deterred. Who wouldn't want those undaunted ones on their team?

The refugees in the camp who did not visit the church became enraged. They continually talked about us in the mosques. Each time, before they threw fire, they would make sure to shut off our water supply from the street. The police always responded, with an increased interest in Bibles and videos. With every fire and persecution, we would bless the Lord for being found worthy to suffer for the gospel.

> So they went on their way from the presence of the Council, rejoicing that they had been considered worthy to suffer shame for his name.
>
> Acts 5:41 (NASB)

We were lying in bed one night when I heard our volunteer, Thomas, scream, "Fire!" At that time, we had two volunteers—a woman from Singapore and a man from the United States. We went outside and witnessed our car being consumed in a ball of flames. Even the steering wheel was in flames. I turned and said to both of them, "Are you thankful? This time, you do not have to clean soot off of walls!" We turned up the music and danced in the street.

We were worshiping the Lord with all our hearts. I did not feel worried, and we were so glad it was not another house fire. As we were rejoicing, we were so high in the Spirit that I felt feathers on the tips of my fingers. I was sure there were angels above us. When the policemen showed up, they thought we had been drinking. We told them we were simply high in the Lord. As they were leaving, they again asked for Bibles.

A prophet came to visit and spoke, "God said do not be upset about the fires the enemy has thrown at you. This is little compared to the fire you will blow back at the enemy in that appointed day."

Losing All

Somehow, my staff and I got invitations to attend the Jerusalem mayor's party for the Feast of Tabernacles outside the municipality. We were all fasting from sugar, coffee, tea, and meat, and we were planning to attend this big event.

I thought, *This is just amazing that we have been invited to this party.* I felt so honored and thought we should definitely plan to attend. Just a few days before the party, the Lord said to me, "Do not touch sugar." I wondered about this because I had already been on this fast for a long time.

I went to the party with the team. It was being held in a beautiful tent at the governmental building in West Jerusalem. A magnificent feast had been laid out before us that seemed to include every dessert you could imagine. My volunteers looked at me and said, "Is it okay to eat this stuff?"

I said, "Sure, why not?"

I walked over and picked up a cookie. I told myself it was a cracker and not a cookie, and it was all right to eat it. As I bit down on this "cracker," a huge dread fell upon me. I realized something terrible had just happened, and I looked for a napkin to spit it out.

After the party was over, we returned to Jericho. We were shocked to discover that our house had been emptied! There were no more laptops, no camera equipment, nothing! Our entire media department had vanished. Within a week, some men from

LeSEA Broadcasting were supposed to come to visit and discuss our launch into television.

When they arrived the following week, they asked to see the media department, so I walked with them into our empty media room. They looked at us and said, "Where is all your media equipment?" I told them it had all been stolen, along with every electronic item in the house. Their faces fell, but they told me, "Do not worry about it. God will give it all back to you." I felt like leaving the mission field and thought about it. The Lord said, "What you run from will surely overtake you."

> Then it shall come to pass, that the sword, which ye feared, shall overtake you there in the land of Egypt, and the famine, whereof ye were afraid, shall follow close after you there in Egypt; and there ye shall die.
>
> Jeremiah 42:16 (KJV)

The lesson I learned from all these tribulations was to chase the giants in the land. When you are chasing the giants, all of heaven fights with you.

I was getting ready to go to London to visit Blake, but my visa had expired. I could barely read the Bible because I was so low in the Spirit. Since everything had been stolen, we had no worship music in the house.

I was crawling out of the land of Israel. I bought a laptop at the airport. When I got to London, I told Blake I was so weak that I felt I needed a couple days to rest. I thought, *If I could only get a copy of the Bible on CD and listen to it.* After finding the nearest store and buying the Psalms and New Testament on CD, I rushed back to my room. As I listened to the word of God on the new computer, I felt like there was water flowing over me once again. After a few days, I was able to really enjoy my time in London with Blake. I knew we had a great destiny in front of us, and I rejoiced as the Comforter flooded me and restored me.

Over the next three months, we began to receive many donations. Christians from all over the world began to send us things. It was amazing how quickly God restored our possessions, including two TV cameras.

The Big Fire

Communion services in our house in Jericho were wondrous. The Spirit always touched the people. A Canadian woman was slain in the Spirit when Rulah, a Palestinian disciple, prayed for her.

That night, however, Eyad told Ahmed and Rulah's mother, Lativa, that our place was going to be hit with a really big firebomb. No one mentioned the fire to me. The team had lined up about one hundred plastic chairs that we used for church outside the window that night. It was a very large picture window in front of our house that had a protective screen with bars on it. I did not know the plastic chairs were made of gasoline, but the terrorists did.

They started a huge fire. The heat of the fire came through the wall and blew out every window in the house, except a small room in the back where we were storing the media equipment. Even the air-conditioners and refrigerator melted in the heat of the fire that blazed through the windows of the house.

Thomas, a volunteer, always seemed to know as soon as a fire hit, because he would hear it. We had prepared an evacuation plan in advance, and we all knew which door to run out of. If we would have waited ten or fifteen minutes, the fire would have been too hot and fierce to run through. As soon as we heard Thomas yell "Fire!" we knew to run outside as fast as we could. Thomas and Shermeen were the most amazing volunteers. They understood that all the fires and tribulations were a sure sign that God was with us.

This time, as soon as we got outside, the police were already there. We were surprised because we had not called them. Sadly, they just stood there and watched as the huge fire burned. My friend, Abraham, came over and said, "You need to leave." He was pleading with us. "You have to get out or they are going to kill you!"

This was not the first time my friends had begged me to leave. After every major fire, church members would come and plead with me to be careful, and many would say it would be better for me to leave.

This time, the damage to the house was so severe that we could not fix it. We did not want to fix it either. With every window gone, it was like a shelled-out building. We hung sheets in place of windows. Everywhere we looked was black with soot. Since no one was willing to rent to us, we lived in that pitiful condition for weeks.

During that time, I was expected to go to speak in Singapore. My volunteers insisted I go because it was going to be a very large conference, but I was struggling with the idea because I didn't want to leave them in such a situation. They kept encouraging me to go. They felt my yes should be yes, and my no should be no. So a week later, I made the decision to go ahead and attend the conference in Singapore. God used Cornerstone Church in Singapore to build me back up, to minister to me, and to encourage me. They treated me with such honor—surely, it is part of our eternal record.

There were three women at a Bible school in Singapore who said, "We are coming back with you to Jericho, no matter what. We are going to help you clean and stay with you. We will help you rebuild."

I kept trying to talk them out of coming, but no matter what I said, they insisted on meeting me in Jericho. They said they did not care that there were no windows and that they would have to sleep on the floor. They were determined to help. My heart was so touched by their love. Those three daughters just wanted to come and serve. They were used by God to bring us into a full restoration.

Meanwhile, there was a man named Joey who planned to come and help with media. I told him about the condition of the house, and he wanted to know what the media room looked like. I told Joey the media room was okay, but there was nothing else left in the house. He said, "That is fine. I am coming. I knew it would be hot soil."

When I returned from Singapore, I rented a car and began looking for another house to rent. Unfortunately, no one wanted to rent to us because we had earned a reputation of having too many fires. We all continued fasting and praying.

Finally, Isaac told me he found a house to rent in Jericho. The owner was a man who lived in Jerusalem, and he had not heard about us. The day I was scheduled to move, I became very sick, and I could not move or even lift my head. My friends Jan and Greg called from Jerusalem and told me they were going to come and help me move. I told them I was too sick to move, but they came anyway. By the time they arrived in Jericho, some of the neighbors had once again thrown a Molotov through the back window of my new rental car. I was so sick, all I could do was lay there. They started boxing things up and took care of what needed to be done. They said, "You are moving today." They moved me by themselves from the refugee camp into the new house. The way God pours out love through his people is deep.

Rulah's Resurrection

Living Bread International Church

Prayer

Meeting at Green Valley

This time, when we moved, the Lord said, "There will be no more fires." Then the Lord told me to rent a wedding hall to hold our church services in each week. I thought, *Lord, we have had death threats and fires, and now you want me to rent a public wedding hall to have a Christian church service?* I knew it could not be Satan, as he would never tell us to do something so courageous.

We rented the Green Valley Wedding Hall, and God filled it. It was such a bold thing to do. The entire city must have been shocked at our boldness, and so were we. At least one hundred Muslims were faithfully attending church. Now located in a public building, we were so expectant that we could not wait to see what the Lord was going to do next.

God did an awesome job for us in public relations. By his Spirit, he gathered Muslims who had an interest in the Bible and Christianity. People would come from around the world to see the miracle for themselves. Muslims from the West Bank would visit our meetings to see the move of God with their own eyes. Our church began to garner worldwide recognition.

After years at the Green Valley Wedding Hall, we no longer hold meetings there. We now have seventeen home churches running and are making disciples to go to the nations. We hope one day to buy land and build them their own church.

For the most part, Muslims who wish to study Christianity in Israel or Palestine are not welcome in local churches. These people really love coming to church, but the leaders are afraid of retaliation. One day, God will give them a pulpit that many will long to visit.

In Jericho, back in those days, the checkpoint was closed, and the people were very restless most of the time. Through the grace of God, the Israeli army allowed me to bring in some hospital beds and aid. The people watched the trucks unload supplies with tears streaming down their faces. Right after that, the man who had been responsible for many of the fire attacks against us sent me a message. He said, "No hard feelings."

I rejoiced as I sent him a message in return, "No hard feelings."

When you forgive those who trespass against you, there is a wonderful release in the Spirit.

> Whenever you stand praying, forgive, if you have anything against anyone, so that your Father who is in heaven will also forgive you your transgressions.
>
> Mark 11:25 (NASB)

At the same time, I was living in my fourth house in Jericho. It was a three-bedroom villa, at least by Jericho standards, and it was the nicest place I had lived in thus far. The house was vulnerable to Molotov cocktails because there was easy access from the next-door neighbor's stairs.

Abraham said, "You have to move or install security. They can easily throw bombs inside through the window."

I replied, "The Lord said there would be no more fires, so I am not going to install any security systems or window guards."

As I walked through the house, the Lord said, "Your next season is going to be with people."

I thought, *Hmm, the fires were not that bad.*

A Bedouin family with eleven children came to visit. Abu Ahmed, the father of the family, said, "The doctors say I have an incurable eye disease, and they can do nothing for me." Then before I could answer, he said, "Mohammad's power is greater than Jesus."

I thought of telling him to let Mohammad heal his eyes. The Lord spoke to me and very clearly told me to tell him, "If this is true, you will never be healed. But if the power of Jesus Christ is greater than Mohammad, by morning, your eye disease will be gone."

The following morning, when Abu Ahmed woke up, his eyes were completely healed.

One day, Lativa and another man brought her daughter, Rulah, to my house and lay her on my floor. They had just returned from the Jericho hospital where they were told there was nothing they could do for her. She was unconscious, and no one knew why. I couldn't tell whether she was breathing or not. Lativa was frantic. She told us we had to take Rulah to the hospital in Jerusalem. The problem was that it was a Saturday. This is the true Biblical appointed time and the official Sabbath day in Israel. Stores and checkpoints were closed on the Sabbath. Practically everything was closed. I called the Israeli liaison officer and told him I had a woman on my floor and explained the situation. We were continually praying for her the entire time.

The Jericho hospital said they could not help, so the Israeli army gave a special clearance for me to drive her through the checkpoint and into Jerusalem. As we drove to the hospital, we prayed for a resurrection of the dead. Lativa went into the hospital and told them that her daughter was in a coma state, but she did not know what had caused it.

Right then, still in the car, Rulah began to open her eyes! The sudden recovery was so dramatic that the doctor thought Rulah might have been crazy and suggested a psychiatrist. As we drove back to Jericho, I convinced the women that Rulah was not crazy. The doctor just did not understand the miraculous power of God.

The next night, we held our weekly church service. Right in the middle of our service, the Israeli army called to make sure that Rulah was okay. Today, if someone preaches about the resurrection at our church services, Rulah always comes forward and wants to share her testimony. She knows in her heart that she was resurrected from the dead and that God did a very great miracle for her.

The Kindness of the Lord

Blake's friend, Suleiman, had now grown to be a young man. He approached me one day and asked if we would be willing to help him financially so that he could attend college. I told him we would help with Bible College, but I refused to send him secretly. I asked for an appointment with his father. I told Suleiman that if his father agreed to this, we would send him to Bible College.

Suleiman made an appointment with his father. I told his father that we wanted to send his son to Bible College, but it had to be with his approval. According to Suleiman, his father had spent seven months naked in an Israeli prison, and he hated Israel. Suleiman wanted to be a peacemaker and not a terrorist. I was sitting with his hard-hearted father, talking about his son, and tears were running down his face. He said, "Of course, it is important that he keeps the ideology of Islam, but I will not forget that you are willing to educate my son."

To me, this was very powerful. The Lord showed me how to break through. Minister to the children, and you can win the hearts of the fathers.

Presidential Breakfast

As we entered another season of acceleration and change, I felt like God was calling me out of the wilderness. By then, I had been in Jericho for nearly five years. We had witnessed deaf ears open, the mute speaking, and a crippled girl walking. It was awesome. People from all over the world were visiting Jericho to see the revival that was taking place. Our services included Muslim Arabs. Every week, something extraordinary would happen, and it was great fun. No more fires, not as many death threats, and things were really good.

To top it off, something happened that I never would have guessed could have happened to me or anyone living in a refugee camp. Thanks to my friends Connie and Bill Wilson, I received an invitation to a presidential breakfast being held during President Bush's term in office. They sent me an official invitation with the presidential seal on it. I was so excited at what the Lord had done. Growing up, I do not remember ever being chosen for anything. I sent a copy to my mom and dad, who were so proud that they showed it to some of their neighbors. I thought, *How wonderful, God, that after all the trials and tribulations, I am going to have breakfast with the president.* I felt something transpiring in the Spirit. The Lord was flooding me with his love and acceptance.

The ministry in Jericho was finally flourishing, but as I was preparing to leave for the presidential breakfast, an imam began speaking out against me in the mosque again. In the past, I would have stayed inside my house and prayed. Now I knew to pray and then go to confront the giants. I sent someone from my team to go talk to him and explain that I was in the middle of packing to go speak with government officials and senators at the presidential breakfast in America about the people of Palestine. The imam was such an extremist that he never spoke anything but Arabic, the "holy language." However, when this imam heard that I was about to go speak about his people with the American government, he let one English word cross his lips—wow. He then sent a message stating he had dropped his case against me, and we had no more trouble from him after that.

The Deliverance of Isaac

Isaac Nuseibeh

Isaac was an elder in our church in Jericho. He had been with me since the very beginning of the outreach in 2003. He was an alcoholic and a former Muslim who was now living for Jesus Christ. He prayed and asked Jesus to strengthen him. Even though Isaac was still drinking every day, I felt he was getting stronger in the Spirit. From 4:00 to 6:00 p.m., while we had church services, he would not drink. Some of our volunteers in Jericho had told me that our reputation was going to be ruined if we did not get rid of Isaac. People from around the world were now coming to visit us, and they were telling me they could smell alcohol on Isaac.

When I had discipleship times with Isaac, he would say, "The Lord is making me stronger every day." I told the team in Jericho that there was no way I was going to the throne of grace and telling God I was worried about our reputation. Vern and Ann, our city managers, serving in Jericho, had so much love flowing through them that I knew they could love Isaac in any condition.

At that time, others suggested we send him to a recovery program. The volunteers asked if I would pay for it, and I answered yes. Isaac planned on going, but at the last minute, he changed his mind. Some of our volunteers thought that Isaac did not want deliverance. At times, the battle was intense.

Six months later, Isaac went to open a can of beer, and Jesus Christ appeared to him. Jesus Christ took the beer from his hand and set it down. He said to Isaac, "That is not who you are." Isaac has never taken a drink since. People thought he would go through massive withdrawal, but he never did. That vision of Jesus was so powerful that Isaac has never wanted to touch alcohol again, no matter how heavy the temptation is.

Nothing is impossible with the Lord. Jesus Christ can set you free from anything. He cares about your situation, no matter how long you have had it or how impossible it looks to men.

Promoted

One day, Rotem, the Israeli liaison officer in Jericho, summoned me for an appointment. He was helping with aid and coordination to the Palestinians. I went into this office and sat down opposite him. He told me, "You are doing a very good work. You do not get involved in politics and are really doing what you say you are doing. It is time for promotion. Take an office in Jerusalem and be registered officially as an NGO. If you can do what you did in Jericho in the other twenty-seven refugee camps, we believe that you can change the face of the nation."

The officer made the arrangements for us to be approved. Before I signed the final paper for a rental house in Jerusalem, a couple of young saints brought me a message from the Lord. I was moving very slowly because the cost of rent in Jerusalem was very high compared to Jericho. The girls visiting said, "God said this is not a step but a leap into the air. Leap into the air, and God will catch you." That was all it took, and I signed the contract and prepared to move to Jerusalem.

I will never forget watching God deliver us from the flames, the people crying with me in the ash heaps, weeping at the kindness of the local nuns who provided me with a hot shower, killing scorpions, the nights we met God on the top of the Mount of Temptations, the love of the Palestinians in the refugee camps, and going without water. No matter what the trial was, God broke through like a flood against my enemies. I will bless his name forever for his goodness and mercies. There are twenty-seven refugee camps in the land. If you like plowing where no one else is working, the Lord may give you a refugee camp to work in.

Blake's Resurrection

While we were preparing to move from Jericho to Jerusalem, a man from London came to the house and said, "I know a ministry in Jerusalem that has a new prayer center. I think your ministry is great, so I will make sure your ministry is put on its prayer list." The guy was very persistent and took all our information. A few days later, he sent me an e-mail to say he was very sorry, but the prayer center did not want to pray for me or our ministry. I did not understand this until a short time later, when God showed me his power and his army. Do not be discouraged when these things happen. When you are following the Lamb, and a door shuts, remember that he always has a greater plan and a greater door.

Five days later, Abu Ali, our Muslim gardener, came to me at seven o'clock in the evening. He gave me eight Israeli candles and said, "Please light five candles. Yeshua said to light five candles. Please, Karen, light five candles. Yeshua, Yeshua."

In one of his earlier visions, the Lord had appeared to him and said, "This woman is a holy woman. You had better take care of this woman." That happened a couple of months after I had moved into the fourth house. Later that night, I was feeling very tired. It was about eleven o'clock, and I was thinking, *Lord, do I really have to light these candles?* The only thing I had for candle holders were some little tiny round silver things that other candles used to be in. I went ahead and lit the five candles and then dozed off.

Later, I noticed one of the candles had fallen to the ground. I felt dread as I looked at the candle that had fallen on the ground. I picked up the candle again and stood it up, but I did not light it. I awakened later to find that the candle had fallen again. This time, it had fallen into another candle. The one candle seemed to be holding up the other one. I thought, *Someone has fallen and the Lord is holding him.*

Shortly afterward, I got a call from a London hospital saying I had to come right away because Blake had been in a serious accident. A big truck had hit him, and he was unconscious. He was in ICU, and the doctors said it was very serious.

I checked the Internet for tickets and realized I could not get a ticket online for a flight taking off in a couple of hours. I drove to the airport and ran up to British Airways and fell on their mercy. I will never forget their kindness. I was on a plane from Israel to London an hour and a half later.

Once I boarded the plane, it was like being in a dream. I was thinking about my son and was upset that I had let him go to London alone. I knew other leaders in the land who had sent their children to Tel Aviv when the kids were not walking with the Lord. I had encouraged my son to go to London. I was feeling so guilty and then frustrated because I thought God had said to let him go.

I decided to blame God. I started with, "God, how could you let this happen? You said if I gave Blake to you, you would take care of him."

God rebuked me very tenderly. He touched my heart and told me, "All is well."

I felt dread and peace at the same time. No matter what, I knew God had never dropped me, nor had he ever been unfaithful. I held on to this word and trusted him.

When I arrived at the hospital in London, Blake was still in a coma in the ICU. The doctors told me to prepare myself, as he may never wake up. They told me that in ten years, he might only be able to blink an eye. They described the quality of life I could expect for Blake; they were preparing me to deal with him being on life support or him being dead. They also said that if he woke up now, they would keep him in a medically induced coma because his brain was swollen and bleeding in four areas. Blake looked so small and helpless in the hospital bed.

A day later, the surgeon told me about a procedure they were going to do to release pressure on his brain. A guy in the next bed had just had a similar surgery, and he looked really bad. Before I arrived, the doctors had already drilled a hole in Blake's head to take a reading because of his swollen brain. I told the surgeon I did not want any surgery done on Blake's brain. I told him God would answer our prayers and bring down the swelling. The doctor said, "We will see about that."

In the ICU, next to my son's bed, I opened my Bible and read out loud. Others who had loved ones in ICU beds would come over and ask me to read to their loved ones too.

The hospital staff would make everyone leave for two hours each day while they performed cleaning duties in the ward. During those two hours, I would run to the Internet cafe and e-mail everyone. From the owner of hardware stores down to my garbage man, I e-mailed everyone on my list to plead for prayer for Blake. The following afternoon, during cleaning, I went to the Internet cafe. The first e-mail I opened was from a French nun in Istanbul whom I had never met. She said she was lighting candles for Blake. Then I received another e-mail from a church I had never heard of. They said they were having a special prayer meeting for my son. Eventually, I got a deluge of e-mails from people who were praying from all over the nations. Most of them were from strangers saying they were praying for my son. Every time I received an e-mail, I forwarded it to my mom and dad. They would cry and say they could not believe that strangers were praying for their grandson. I believe that tragedy brought my parents closer to the Lord.

The Lord spoke to me through all that and said, "My army has risen."

I have never loved the body of Christ more than I did at that moment. God raised up his army of people to pray for Blake, and we did not even know most of them. But God surely knew who they were. I was so proud to be part of God's great army. During that time, e-mails were continuously flowing in with prayers for Blake, and I knew that God could do what men could never do. I might not have made it on man's list, but the King sure had me on his list and in a greater plan.

The doctors came to me and said, "Blake's brain is bleeding in four areas, his neck is broken, and his spine is fractured. Right now, it appears the swelling in his brain is going down." He tried to tell me maybe the original reading on his machine had been wrong. I rejoiced at the response of God through prayer. The doctor said, "You cannot expect anything. We may need to do a tracheotomy."

I looked around as they rolled dead bodies out of ICU and thought, *The gates of hell will never prevail. Life is stronger than death, and God is surely the author of life! He is a God of promise, and I will trust in him forever to deliver my son out of the dungeon of death.* The next night, I was praying late into the night at my son's bedside when I thought I saw him move. I rejoiced! I knew he wanted to wake up. I felt I could hear him say, "I am tired of being drunk." At that moment, a nurse named James came to Blake's bed. He also saw him move, and immediately, he gave my son three injections of various drugs. Then he turned the medicine gauge up really high. I had felt Blake was just about to wake up and then this happened. I felt sick to my stomach, and I had to get out of the hospital. I sat on my bed and just screamed. Then I called the hospital and said to James, "Why are you injecting drugs into my son when we waited so long for him to come out of the coma? My son wants to wake up."

James said, "It is better if it happens on another shift."

The next day, I was like a wild woman as I asked everyone to stop the medications. I went from one nurse to another and from doctor to doctor. Finally, one doctor said that I might be right. The doctor ordered them to take Blake off the medicine.

Blake woke up, looked at me, and said, "Nurse?"

For the next few hours or so, he kept calling me nurse.

After he called me nurse again, I held my Bible up to my face and said, "Do nurses carry around Bibles?"

He looked up at me and said, "Mom!"

The doctors said his neck was broken, his spine was fractured, and that he might never walk again. I realized at this point that when they cannot see it, they really do not give any hope. I knew it was best to listen to the voice of God and not of those doctors. They had no hope for anything.

One of the doctors said, "I will not know how bad the broken neck is until I take the brace off." He took the brace off, and Blake moved his neck. Previously, he had taken five x-rays. Each one showed Blake's neck was broken, but now his neck was healed. The doctor said, "I don't know what's going on here. I should be documenting this, but I just don't know what to say."

I knew in my heart exactly what was going on. His name is Jesus Christ, and he conquered death, hell, and the grave. Piece by piece, he was putting my boy back together again.

Blake was awake, and I rejoiced in the resurrection power of the Lord. His neck was not broken, but he still had no control over the lower part of his body. His limbs would not work, and he was like a noodle. I longed to take Blake back with me to Israel as fast as they would allow.

The wheelchairs they had in this brain trauma center were not very nice, so I was going around the hospital, trying to find Blake the best one. Finally, a man who was leaving the hospital gave me his really nice wheelchair. I told Blake, "Look what I found for you."

Some of Blake's street friends were coming to see him at the hospital, and he loved being pushed around in his wheelchair. Much of his memory was gone, but he was talking now. The doctors asked me what my house was like in Israel. Could it accommodate a wheelchair? Could I get him the therapy that he needed? I answered, "Of course."

I was so happy my son was coming home. Blake told me that before the accident, the Lord had appeared to him a few times and said to him, "Go help your mother."

I asked Blake, "Why didn't you tell me about this?"

He said he had not wanted to rush anything. The fear of God fell on me as he told me those things.

Every time I went to the hotel to try and get some sleep, Blake would call me and ask where I was. The hotel was just across the street from the hospital, so one time, when he called, I told him that, trying to reassure him that I was not far off. Then I heard him get out of his bed while trying to look out the window to see me. His limbs were too weak, and he did not have the coordination to walk. I could hear his head hit the floor with a thud, and my heart hit the floor with him. After this, no one tried to get him to walk because his brain and limbs were obviously not connected.

Blake could not do anything by himself. I began to be really aggravated in the Spirit. I was saying to God, "You raised him from the dead. Now I have to bring him home in a wheelchair?" I thought, *Is the devil ripping me off?* My heart felt that God surely had more miracles in store.

One night, Blake had two or three friends visiting him in the hospital. He said, "Mom, I have to go to the bathroom."

I said to his friends, "Can you help my son walk to the bathroom?"

Blake looked over at me and asked, "Mamma, can I walk?"

I said, "Son, you can walk! In the name of Jesus Christ, you can walk!"

He jumped out of his chair, and it looked like a strut came into his walk. I felt like I was watching a movie. It was fantastic!

Not long afterward, we walked out of the hospital. God had delivered my son from the mouth of the lion and from sure death. No matter what fire, death threat, disease, or oppression you are going through, God is greater. He is the Lord of breakthroughs, and he will always rescue you. Do not ever give up!

The City of the Great King

Blake Davis just released from the hospital with his mother,
Pastor Karen at the Jordan River

Blake Davis

Mike

Blake and I flew back to Israel from London. We had made plans to move to Jerusalem, and blessings were overtaking us from every corner of the earth. We could feel the favor as God kept opening doors. Now that we were officially registered as an NGO, ministries that had been silent for years began to show an interest in us. I was suddenly being invited to have lunch or dinner with leaders in Jerusalem. I really felt like God was carrying me through a coming-out party in the Spirit. The call to Jericho had been a very lonely one in fellowship, but the Lord is faithful, and his bond is closer than a friend. The move to Jerusalem was amazing. To have come through Jericho, the door of the land, into the city of the great King was more than words can describe. It was exhilarating, and I felt gratitude to the Lord. To be living in the city of the great King was a huge blessing. I was so thankful, and I knew this had come through those years of schooling in the Spirit in Jericho.

As soon as we moved to Jerusalem, we hired a young guy named Mike to work for our ministry. He was an outcast from his father's church. My son had also been fired from the media department at one of the local churches because they had been told he was not living a godly life. Out of concern for their reputation, the management approached him at work and said, "You have to leave because of your sinful life."

I could feel their pain, and my heart was bleeding for both of them. Some of the things we do to each other in the name of Jesus Christ can be brutal.

Sometimes, God brings you to this position to show you to trust and lean only on him. People will drop you, they will betray you, and they will let you down, but the Lord will never let you fall too far before his arm catches you. If you are going through something like this, know that the Lord's love never fails, and he is always there for you.

The Lord had told me to disciple Mike, but before long, I was receiving calls from local pastors who were telling me to get rid of him. They were saying I should not have other young people around this boy, as he was a bad influence. The Lord told me, "Keep him like he is your own son and disciple him. I want you to love this son."

While we were filming B-roll on the Mount of Temptations, we had a visitor from London named Paul. Paul prophesied a blessing over Mike and said, "The Lord has given your father thousands, but he is going to give you tens of thousands. Mike, you are going to outrun your father."

From that day forward, a prophetic word was driving Mike and pulling him into his destiny. I knew he would be a great one for God, and I loved him dearly.

Mike had a friend named Matan who was doing something called national service, which some young Israelis do instead of serving in the army. One day, Matan was fired from the charitable job he had been working at to fulfill his service, so the government official asked us to hire him. We did not have to pay his wages as the Israeli government paid him. I told Matan we were going to use him to drum while we worship. Matan is a great drummer, and every morning, he and Mike would play the drums while I read the Bible. Matan also wrote music for our TV show. I had other pastors' kids as volunteers, but they were just passing through and not long-term.

One day, while just the three of us were at the house, I told Mike we needed to do Communion. I told Matan, "Mike and I are going to do Communion, and you are welcome to join us if you like. If not, you can watch us."

> So Jesus said to them, "Truly, truly, I say to you, unless you eat the flesh of the Son of Man and drink his blood, you have no life in yourselves. He who eats my flesh and drinks my blood has eternal life, and I will raise him up on the last day."
>
> John 6:53–54 (NASB)

I explained Jesus Christ was the living bread that came down out of heaven and gave life to the dead. Matan thought about my words and said, "I would like to see what it's like to do Communion with you and Mike."

> For my flesh is true food, and my blood is true drink.
>
> John 6:55 (NASB)

Matan was following along with me in his Hebrew Bible. He looked at Mike and me and said, "I wondered how you people got it in you."

My heart was so blessed at the revelation. Mike was now radically transforming before my eyes, and I was so proud of him. He had a crucial role in helping with the growth of the organization. We had meetings running with liaison officers all over the country as we coordinated travel through the checkpoints and aid to the poor. We learned to pierce the heart of terror with Christian educational materials, including forgiveness and peace.

Mike was outstanding among the volunteers, and he willing to do whatever I asked of him. I knew that one day, he would accomplish much for the kingdom of God.

Resurrection of a Mother and Baby

When we moved our headquarters to Jerusalem, we still continued to minister and hold church services in Jericho. One day, we went to Jericho to give away food. We went over to the house of a woman who was a member of our church, although she came without her husband's knowledge. Her husband was an Islamic extremist. I knew she was pregnant, and I wanted to see if the baby had been born yet because we had baby supplies to give her.

When we arrived at her house, her husband began testifying about the birth of their new son. He was clearly shaken, and could barely speak English, but we were able to understand him. "When I got to the hospital, the doctors said, 'Either your wife or your baby will die. It's up to you to decide. You must choose which one to save.'"

He said he had told the doctor he wanted to save his wife, so they performed a C-section. The cut was about a foot long, and she lost so much blood that she died on the operating table. As she lay there, dead, she saw Jesus standing next to her, praying for her life. The Bible says he lives to make intercession.

> Therefore he is able also to save forever those who draw
> near to God through him, since he always lives to make
> intercession for them.

Hebrews 7:25 (NASB)

As Jesus was praying for her, she felt her life come back to her body. She looked over at her baby boy, and she knew he was dead. She watched Jesus walk over and put his hand on the boy as the baby came back to life.

We were amazed to hear this testimony from her militant husband. He insisted on naming the baby boy Jesus. Jesus Christ gave him back his wife and baby, and we rejoiced as this Muslim testified to this very fact.

By that time, Living Bread was an official NGO in Israel. When we signed up for the NGO status with the State of Israel, we were truthful about everything our ministry was doing. We told them we were using Arabic Bibles for our educational ministry and that our television show was in English with Arabic subtitles. We said we used Christian principles in our teachings and in our outreach of anti-terror education, along with feeding the poor. We would have to write another book to tell you all that the Lord did to topple terror in the city of Jericho.

During that first year and a half in Jerusalem, I became an itinerant speaker, and I went on speaking tours around the world. One day, I was speaking at a Methodist church, and Monica, one of Tampa Bay's judges, was in the audience. Afterward, Monica invited us all out to lunch.

Later, Monica contacted me again. She said, "I am praying about coming to work for you in Jerusalem." Shortly after that, the Lord told Monica to resign as a judge. He told her she would be my assistant in Jerusalem.

I felt in my heart that the Lord wanted me to tell her to bring her gavel. I was sure the Lord wanted to use her to decree righteous judgments. I learned so much from this woman. I learned how to make declarations, about integrity in the court, and about the Righteous Judge ruling on behalf of the poor and needy.

We have an ongoing worship watch in Jerusalem, where we make declarations and decrees according to the heart of God and what he is releasing upon the earth.

> Then I will restore your judges as at the first, and your counselors as at the beginning; after that you will be called the city of righteousness, a faithful city.
>
> Isaiah 1:26 (NASB)

Trying to Buy the Land

Project Gilgal and the Mount of Temptation Jericho

A couple gave us a very large sum of money to help us buy land in either Jericho or Hebron. They were both on their knees, saying, "God said if we make it happen for his children, that he will make it happen for our own children." As the negotiation fell through in Jericho, we immediately tried to buy a piece of property in Hebron. Suddenly, out of nowhere, others wanted to buy the property also. God made us pull out when Christians began bidding against each other. The high bidder never closed the deal, and we found out later that no one can buy land in the Palestinian area without a license. references to large amounts, which are better given in numerals and currency symbol

In the early days, our meetings with the Palestinian government were not easy. We paid a lawyer $6,000 to set up the deal for us for us. He insisted that we pay the full amount up front. After getting the final approval, he told us to pick up our license on Monday.

The day we arrived, he said there was no license and that we would never get one. The funds we had given him were gone. At times, the Palestinian officials would tell us to leave Jericho, and on other occasions, they would commend us for the work we were doing. The Lord had told us he would get us the license, so we kept trying. One of the Palestinian leaders said, "We can never license that organization because of the woman who talks about Jesus all the time."

Another official said, "Who cares if she talks about Jesus Christ? She is feeding our children and creating many wonderful programs for our poor."

The Lord said, "Take care of the people. Be generous."

Because of the large donation of that couple, we became extravagant givers to the poor in the land. The love and kindness of the Lord brought about repentant hearts.

We broke bread with the people, prayed for their babies, rebuilt their houses, trained them with job skills, taught them English, started a milk program for the babies, made a book bag program for children whose fathers were in prison, gave counseling to the abused, provided welfare to the hungry, and offered peacemaking programs to those who wanted life without terror, and they welcomed us with open arms.

We are now licensed in the Palestinian territory, and we bless the Lord for the huge door only he could have opened. Our license never expires, and we can now buy land. In the Palestine region, this is impossible without the Lord.

Gilgal is the land in Jericho that we pray will one day be home to the Living Bread International Church. Jericho is the doorway to the promised land. According to the Scriptures, that is where Joshua and all of Israel camped when they first came across the Jordan River after spending forty years in the wilderness. That is the point of blessing where it all began in the exceedingly good land. The manna stopped, Israel was circumcised, and Israelites began to eat the fruit of land in that place.

> Now the people came up from the Jordan on the tenth of the first month and camped at Gilgal on the eastern edge of Jericho.
>
> Joshua 4:19 (NASB)

I asked the Lord why I had needed to spend five years living in Jericho before moving to Jerusalem. He spoke and said, "I am bringing you through the door of the land."

Today, some Jewish people from the local kibbutz have asked us to represent them for relationship talks with their Palestinian neighbors in Jericho. We have invested years in ministering to the Palestinians. We have also worked very closely with the Israelis and have a glorious freedom flowing between two peoples in the land. We believe in one God, one kingdom, and one King.

> Blessed are the peacemakers, for they shall be called sons of God.
>
> Matthew 5:9 (NASB)

Rome

Rome Prophetic Tour

I loved touring Jerusalem and was especially interested in places in the land where the glory of God had moved. I began to meditate on continuing where the early church had left off. The early church had such power and was a bold witness for Jesus

Christ. I longed for the freedom they had to soar like an eagle and be radical for him.

Our second location in Jerusalem was on a street called Angel in Light. I could see Mount Zion from the porch. Once, as I was staring at Mount Zion, I had a vision of the martyrs in the Colosseum in Rome waving silver relay sticks in the air. The vision went very deep inside of me, and I booked tickets for Rome. I could not wait to stand in the Colosseum and pick up a relay stick. I knew I was going to have an encounter with the Lord.

When I arrived in Rome, I went to the Colosseum and waited upon the Lord. In my mind, I could see the martyrs holding up silver relay sticks. A stick appeared in front of my face, and I could read the words *Greater Works* engraved on it.

The Lord said, "They are waiting for my people to run their portion of the race."

I realized that they were being held back as they were crying out for us to finish the race.

Our destiny was wrapped up in the destiny of the cloud of witnesses and those that had given their lives for the gospel.

> Because God had provided something better for us, so that apart from us they would not be made perfect.
>
> Hebrews 11:40 (NASB)

I was expecting great things as I entered the prison where historians believe Paul and Peter may have been together while waiting for execution. They say Paul was beheaded, as he was a Roman citizen, and it was against the law to crucify him. Some historians believe Peter was crucified upside down. The interior of the prison was damp and dark, although it has been remodeled since then. I reflected on waiting for execution. To be made willing by the Spirit to pay any price for the gospel was what I desired. I knew if the historians were correct, this was the area of the exit for both of these apostles. It was a great place to pick up a relay baton in the Spirit.

My friend said, "My hair is standing up. What is happening?"

I was in a trancelike state, and I could feel his presence and anointing so close to me that I could not move. I saw the white robes of the Lord next to me. He slid what looked like a rain stick in my hand. As I felt the pressure of it go into my hand, I could not speak or move. Later, as we left to go up the stairs, I heard the Lord speak. He said, "Do not rebuild it. Begin where they left off."

Church in Jerusalem

Living Bread International Church Jerusalem

One morning, Isaac wanted to meet us at the Damascus Gate of the Old City, where he told us about a vision the Lord gave him while he was in Jericho. Isaac showed us a building near the gate that he had seen in the vision and said, "God wants you to start a church here."

I was kind of laughing to myself. As busy as we all were, now God wanted me to start a church in Jerusalem? But I took one look at Isaac, and I knew he had seen the Lord.

I told Isaac, "Whatever it costs, we will take this building and be obedient to the vision God has given you." I knew in my heart that God wanted to do something for the Arab people who wanted to know about him.

We rented the building and opened a church. One evening, as we worshiped, an Arab man walked in. As he looked around, the people looked familiar to him. He came up to me and said, "I have already seen every one of you in a vision. God told me to come here to learn about Jesus Christ."

I was so encouraged at the many testimonies such as his that came to us and showed us that God was doing the work by his Spirit.

Not long after our church opened, the Lord spoke to me and said, "Carry a mandate to prophesy."

We are located just one block from the Garden Tomb, and we love declaring with all Jerusalem, "Blessed is he who comes in the name of the Lord." We also use the church as our corporate office and television studio. The Lord told me that a spiritual move of God would pour out of this place, and we are expecting it. We will tarry in Jerusalem until we have been clothed with power from on high. As the Lord lives, it will surely happen.

Door of Hope TV Show

Karen Dunham broadcasting on the internet

Our TV show, *Door of Hope*, was aired weekly throughout the good land and in other nations as well. One day, I received a letter from a man named David who wanted to see me. In the letter, David explained he was a Jew living in Tel Aviv. Later, when I spoke with him on the phone, he explained to me that he was addicted to our television show. He watched it every Saturday morning at ten o'clock. If he missed it, he said he was really disappointed. David met with me and shared his testimony with me. He told me that while living in Tel Aviv, he decided to become a Christian. He found a church and was baptized. Then he was told he could no longer be a Jew because he was a Christian.

I told him, "David, even though you believe in Jesus Christ, you are still a Jew. You will never stop being a Jew. The early church members were all Jews who believed in Christ, but still Jews. Jesus Christ was a Jew." Then I said, "Our television show is in English with Arabic subtitles because it ministers to Arabs. What was it that made you watch it every week?"

David smiled as he said, "I never met anyone whose God loved everybody. I could feel and see by the way you spoke on your TV show that your God loves everyone. That is when I decided I wanted your God to be my God!"

Later, David attended one of our church services. I instructed everyone in the church to lay hands on him and bless him. That day, a young man named Mohammad, who was of the Islamic faith, was present in church. After we blessed David, I called Mohammad to come up for prayer. When we began to pray for Mohammad, David came back up and said, "Please, can I pray for Mohammad?"

He prayed blessings for Mohammad in Hebrew.

Then Mohammad said, "Could I pray a blessing for David?"

Mohammad prayed a blessing over David in Arabic.

That day, I knew in my heart that nothing was impossible with God.

One day, we received an e-mail from a man in Iran. He had been watching our television show and wrote that they had all been lied to. He said, "We thought you hated us, but I can see by your TV show that it was all a lie." At that moment, I realized how amazing God was and how he can invade any territory.

A Jewish man named Perry Baker was serving a life sentence without parole in the Iowa state prison. After watching us on TV in 2006, he sent us a letter along with a donation of five hundred dollars to support feeding the Palestinians. This caught my attention, as I knew how hard it was to get funds in and out of prison.

Later, I made a TV show thanking Perry Baker for funding the move of the Spirit in Jerusalem. The Lord had me prophesy and pray for him on television. The next year, on a speaking tour in the United States, I decided to visit Perry Baker in prison. Perry had been in prison for years, and he had not had any visitors.

When he came into the room to visit with me, Perry said, "I cannot believe you are here. I will never forget your visit and what your television show did for me." Perry then shared a great testimony that made me weep at God's goodness.

Perry told me, "When you live life in prison with no hope for parole, you tend not to care about things like you would if you thought you had a chance to get out." Perry had given his life to the Lord and was studying the word of God in prison. However, he was still involved in buying and selling drugs to other inmates.

One day, Perry overdosed on a kilo of cocaine and was taken to the hospital. The machine flatlined. As Perry lay dying in the hospital, he asked God to give him fifteen more years like God had done for Hezekiah in Isaiah 38:5. The Lord answered his cry for help and healed Perry. Perry then returned to prison. At the sentencing, they sent him to the "black hole" for a year and a half. The black hole was a solitary confinement where they only brought prisoners out for an hour or two of fresh air, once or twice a week. There was no social contact with anyone in the black hole. After a while in that place, Perry thought he was losing his mind. Then the prison officials brought him a television.

One night, at midnight, Perry watched our television show *Door of Hope*. He said life shot into his body as he heard me say, "Pray for Perry Baker in the prison." I had then prophesied, "Perry, the Lord is the God of the impossible and can open a door no man can shut. The Lord is for you, Perry Baker." Perry said he could not believe he was hearing his name called, and at that moment, he had known the Lord was still with him. So as I sat there visiting with him at the prison, Perry said, "After hearing my name called, everything changed."

Can you hear the Lord calling your name?

Gaza War

Gaza War

With the people

Sharing family pictures

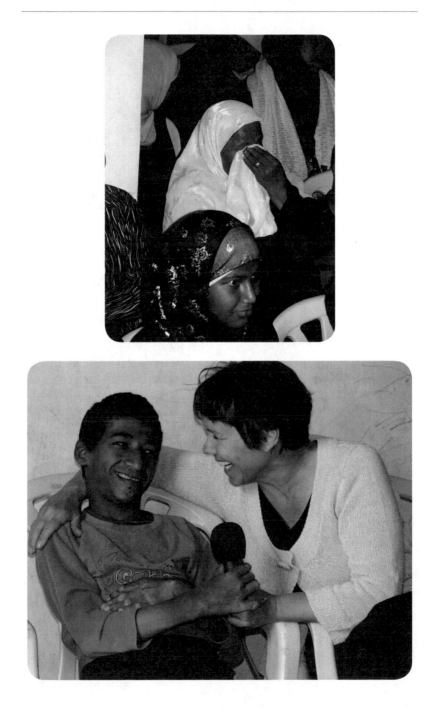

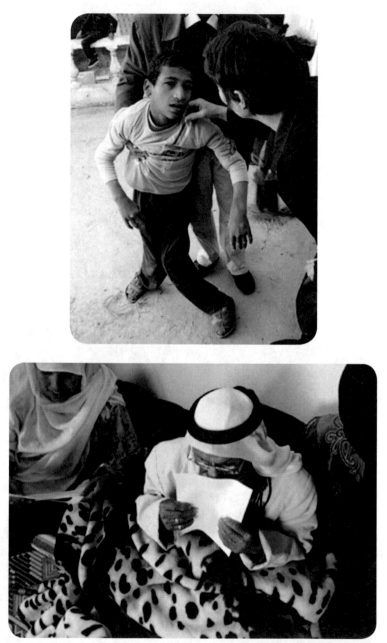

Pictures of Jericho family members being shared with Gaza relatives

Aladdin, Blake and friends painting life on the walls

Painting life

Karen Dunham and Sabreem

Gaza tunnels

International workshop in Turkey

In 2008, we started a prayer meeting in Jericho for Gaza. Thirty or forty members attending our church had families in Gaza, and we gave them special attention. I felt the Lord say, "Go to Gaza and meet their families." We wanted to go to every single family in Jericho that had a relative in Gaza and film them saying hello. We had videos showing their homes, their new babies, and their children, along with a personal message. We took digital images of the families and special gifts to share with their loved ones in the Gaza strip.

We went in and out of refugee camps throughout the Gaza Strip, from the northern part all the way down to the Rafah border in the south. Along with the family video, we took bags of aid and Arabic Bibles. People cried when we arrived at their houses. They asked why Christians would ever do this kind act. The people said there was no amount of money or words to thank the Christians for doing this for the people of Gaza. This birthed a new program in the ministry called Family Connections, which is still in operation today.

In the area of Rafah inside Gaza, we met a fourteen-year-old boy who was crippled and did not have a wheelchair. When he needed to be transported from place to place, his family had to drag him on the ground. His entire body was covered with cuts and bruises. The father told me that his other son was a martyr. They told us that because they received martyr's income, the government would not help the crippled boy in addition to that.

There are many stories like that one in the twenty-seven refugee camps in the land. Frustration and hatred fester, and tools for terrorism develop in places such as these. The camps are unplowed fields and a great place to bring hope to the hopeless with the good news.

In another house, I gave an old man a picture of his son who was living in Jericho. The man began kissing the picture and weeping. Meanwhile, our media team was filming him kissing the picture of his son and weeping over it. We could feel his pain.

As we headed back to Jerusalem, we learned that the old man had died. We went into Jericho and gave the video to the son. The son viewed it and sobbed. I said, "Look how good God is. He gave you and your father one last moment together. It is the mercy of God that we were able to bring you this video. Your father was given that one last moment to think of you before he died."

We visited another family who lived in the Khan Younis refugee camp. They said that during the war, a large part of the family had been gathered in the house. Their nine-year-old boy had pleaded with the family to get out of the house. He kept saying, "We have to get out now!" The boy would not stop. They decided to take the entire family to the uncle's house. Just as they left, the house was blown up. All of them were saved. I rejoiced at our Living God that responds to the prayers of his people.

During our first few trips into Gaza, we stayed at a local hotel along the shores of the Mediterranean Sea. In the front yard of the hotel, they showed us a spot where a seventy-five-pound bomb landed but did not go off. Other hotels and many buildings were blown up. I had taken a suitcase full of Jesus videos and another one full of Bibles with me. In Gaza, we purchased a truck full of aid to deliver to the homes. I gave one of the young men at the hotel a Jesus video and then we went out to meet the families. While I was out, I thought about how I may have endangered the young man's life by handing him the Jesus video. After all, we were in Hamas territory. We delivered our aid and returned to the hotel in the early evening. Men were gathered in the lobby, watching a movie. As we got closer, we were amazed—they were watching the Jesus video! The man at the hotel said, "Do you have any more stories on video about Jesus?"

I said, "Not on me, but I will try to bring you some more."

We heard so many stories of survival from the people whom the church in Jericho had prayed for during the war. The people appeared to be in trauma right after the Gaza War. One young man said there was no hope for the people of Gaza. He said, "I wanted to be a pilot, but no one in the world will train Palestinians to fly."

We heard many touching stories, yet at that time, Gilad Shalit, an Israeli soldier who had been abducted by Hamas, was still being held captive somewhere in Gaza. As my son and I walked the streets one day, we came to a large UN compound across the street from the Islamic University of Gaza. My son looked at me and said with wonder, "Mom, is the Israeli soldier around here?"

Instantly, the hair on my arms stood up, and I heard the Lord say, "He is under that building." Over a million people were being confined because of the terrorist activities and the kidnapped soldier. The soldier, Gilad Shalit, was being held hostage in a tunnel underneath a building in the Gaza Strip and God had just told us. As soon as we were out of Gaza, we met with liaison officers of the Israeli army and eventually the Deputy of Gaza. We were able to tell the Israeli army where their missing soldier was being held. The Lord gave a loud witness with chills, and our hair standing up on our arms as we shared. It was really amazing to use the prophetic gift of God, to speak to a nation in a crisis situation. Soon afterward, the army arranged for the release of one thousand Palestinian prisoners in exchange for their beloved officer, Gilad Shalit. The people of Gaza were happy to see this Israeli soldier go, in hopes that one day the gates to Gaza would be open for them too.

The walls of Gaza were covered with graffiti images depicting death, destruction, revenge, hate, and anger against Israel. Blake initiated a graffiti project in Gaza. He wanted to paint messages of life on the walls of Gaza.

One day, while in Gaza City, politicians were gathering in a building where the back end had been blown off during the war. Blake wanted to paint on the wall. He and Aladdin, a Gazan man we were working with, went inside to get permission. The place was full of people, and the mayor said to come back later. Blake said, "I cannot. I need permission now." He told Blake to write on a piece of paper what he wanted to spray on the walls. Blake wrote on the paper, "Life to Gaza City" and "Peace to the Middle East."

The man, who was a Hamas official, said, "Have fun, son, but do not write *peace* on our walls." As Blake began to paint, traffic stopped, people gathered around him, and he was invited to do a workshop at the local university. An international news agency asked Blake if he would do a story for them, and there was an amazing amount of activity around him as he sprayed the walls in the Gaza strip with a message of life.

The UN offices in the Gaza strip have used artists to paint the front of their walls. We noticed Hamas also had artists paint the walls in the strip with hostile messages.

Afterward, Blake asked me, "What happened, Mom? Why all the traffic and attention?"

I told him that when he wrote *life* on the walls, everything began to change. We presented the school leaders a few program initiatives to encourage the students. Their favorite option was the graffiti initiative. Today, Blake has been asked to paint a wall in every school in the Gaza Strip. I am very proud of my son.

Meeting people where they are at is what God is all about. Blake has done some outstanding graffiti projects in schools throughout the West Bank. He also conducts workshops for children and Painting for Peace projects. Blake's team of local graffiti artists painted a prayer wall for us in our church in Jerusalem. People e-mail us or come in person to write their name on our walls. We love hearing the testimonies that come back to us as we hold up the names written on the walls of the church in prayer. (To add your name to the wall, e-mail us at info@ livingbreadchurch.com or come visit us in Jerusalem, Israel.)

When I was finally ready to leave Gaza, I still had fifty Bibles left. At that time, we did not have a house or an office in the Gaza Strip, so I passed them in a suitcase to a lady named Sabreem, who lived in a refugee camp in Gaza. I said, "You can give the Bibles to your neighbors."

When I returned to Gaza, Sabreem returned my empty suitcase. I looked at her with surprise and asked, "What happened to the Bibles?"

Her face broke into a huge grin as she said, "I gave one to every neighbor. They are waiting for you to come tell them more about what they are reading in the Bible."

The harvest is ready for those who can see the white fields.

One morning, at breakfast in the Palestine Hotel in Gaza, several hotel workers asked me if I would pray for their babies. Our witness does not go unnoticed as we go about doing the work of the kingdom. Through our translator, Mohammad, I asked them, "Do you want to give your babies to the Lord?" I told them the Bible story about Hannah in 1 Samuel 1. Mohammad read the scriptures to the waiters and the workers, and they listened intently. The workers in the hotel said yes. They all wanted to dedicate their children to the Lord. The next time I went into Gaza, I brought certificates of baby dedication, and we prayed over many children.

Later that day, I had a meeting with local Gaza schoolteachers. They wanted to know if we would help them. They all showed an interest in finding a way to remove feelings of hate, vengeance, and murder from the students' hearts. Suddenly, one of them said, "Can you explain baptism to us?" I looked at Blake, and he looked back at me. We had not even been talking about Jesus Christ. I began discussing baptism with them.

Mohammad looked at me and asked, "Shall I tell them the story of Hannah?"

I said, "Great!"

Mohammad opened his Bible and started reading the story of Hannah.

Blake told me, "Mom, you say one word, and they all want to get in the boat."

One of the men asked us if we would like to see the Egyptian border. We said okay. I had no idea what we were about to be shown.

We drove along the Egyptian border, and the driver said, "These are the tunnels. You must be a member of Hamas to own one of them. Inside the tents, there is a pulley system that goes through a tunnel into Egypt. In Egypt, there is a homeowner using his house with a pulley system in it, to export from." You would be amazed at what all comes through the tunnels. Vegetables, wives, and electronics are some of the imports. The driver told us that Hamas had super tunnels that were big enough for automobiles. He also they brought in cash, explosives, and weapons through the tunnels.

We were shocked to be given a tour of those tunnels and kept praying silently that there would be no explosions on that day.

We successfully gathered the Gaza Strip schoolteachers and taught against extreme ideology using Christian principles.

I went into town to buy a refrigerator. The shopkeeper told me I had to wait a couple of few hours for the new ones coming up through the tunnels from Rafah, which is the main entry of goods from Egypt into Gaza. Later, he told me they had a new tunnel being opened from Egypt and that the appliances would be in Gaza City that evening. I waited in my office for my new refrigerator. I was amazed when they delivered it because even though it was new, there were little dents all over it. I thought to myself, *My mother would never accept this scratched and dented refrigerator.* I laughed and thanked the shopkeeper for my new appliance.

The people in Gaza do not have electricity eight hours a day. We hold Bible studies by candlelight, and many nights, we eat dinner the same way. It was very quiet when the electricity went out. I cherish my quiet times with God during power outages.

As we walked out of Gaza, my son said, "Mom, I feel so light." Earlier he had stated that everything inside of you comes to the surface when you are in Gaza. Walking out of Gaza, the weight of the glory of God was so heavy on us that I could feel my entire body in light. I felt like I was wearing boots of glory. I said to one of our volunteers, "Only a foolish person would think you could accomplish all these things that only God could do in just a few days by the power of his Spirit." Surely, it had not been us working these past few days, but him who lives inside of us, opening doors and making a way in the wilderness.

As I left, I gave Rabah, one of the schoolteachers, a Bible and told him to read the book of John. Rabah's uncle is one of the founders of Islamic Jihad. His family name is also one of the top names associated with terror in the Middle East. Back in Jerusalem, I opened an e-mail from Rabah. He said, "I am now one of the born again ones that the book of John talks about."

We are now doing international workshops with Palestinian schoolteachers from Gaza and Israel. We also bring Muslims and Jewish people together in reconciliation meetings. We are in awe and wonder of what God will release on the earth next. We cannot wait and live moment by moment in great expectancy.

Bringing people together in the true peace that only the King can give is a great part of the Living Bread International Church.

Ganges River of India

The body is wrapped with cow dung for luck

We were prophesying nightly in Jerusalem when I announced to the team, "This is really wild, but the Lord just told me to go on a Hindu high place tour in India."

We went to the holiest city of Hinduism—Varanasi, India. Every practicing Hindu wants to die in Varanasi or have ashes sent there. They believe the doorway to paradise is through a part of the Ganges River in Varanasi that they call Mother God.

In the spring of 2010, Blake, Mike, and I went to India. I took my judge's gavel and scrolls. In the book of Jeremiah, he commanded Seraiah to read all the words of Jeremiah 50–51 when he got to the Euphrates River. He then told him to tie them on a rock and throw them in the river.

> Now it shall be, when you have finished reading this book, that you shall tie a stone to it and throw it out into the Euphrates. Then you shall say, 'Thus Babylon shall sink and not rise from the catastrophe that I will bring upon her.'
>
> Jeremiah 51:63–64a (NKJV)

The Lord told me to print a piece of paper with all of Jeremiah chapters 50 and 51 on it. After making numerous copies, we folded them into small scrolls and threw them into the waterway as the Lord directed us.

> And he said to me, "The waters which you saw, where the harlot sits, are peoples and multitudes and nations and tongues."
>
> Revelation 17:15 (NASB)

> Then a strong angel took up a stone like a great millstone and threw it into the sea, saying, "So will Babylon, the great city, be thrown down with violence, and will not be found any longer."
>
> Revelation 18:21 (NASB)

We joined with heaven as we tossed his word into the international waterways and declared that Babylon had fallen and would never rise again. That assignment had the blessings of the King all over it. It is so exciting to serve the Lord. Be faithful with small assignments, and he will give you mighty ones.

On our way to India, we were delayed by authorities and had to remain in Istanbul for a few days. It was an amazing time ordained by God. We stood in the middle of a bridge where the Golden Horn River flowed between Istanbul and Europe and tossed our scrolls into two continents. With one foot in Europe and the other one in Asia, we declared that his enemy, Babylon, was falling and would never rise again.

At Varanasi, we rented a boat to row us down the Ganges River. We made declarations along the way, saying, "Babylon is fallen" as we prophesied and threw scrolls into the waterways. We also saw priests worship fire along the shores and dead bodies floating in the water. People were getting baptized in the river next to decaying bodies.

The city sewage drains into the Varanasi River, which they call Mother God. We saw smoking stakes along the banks, and the driver of the boat explained that they were crematories. The families were chanting to the Hindu gods as the dead bodies burned.

I asked, "Why are bodies floating in the river if they are cremated?"

He answered, "When pregnant mothers die, they tie them to a brick and throw them in the river rather than burn them."

I asked, "What happens to the bodies?"

He answered, "They wash up on the other shore."

I had him take us to the other shore. When we got out of the boat, there were decaying bodies on the shoreline that were being eaten by dogs.

The man explained to us, "They take all the sick dogs with rabies and put them on the island to eat the bodies. This is the gateway to paradise."

I said, "This is what they call paradise?" I realized we were in a gate of hell.

I said to the team, "Take a look. This is a picture of hell."

Blake asked me, "What is the good report about this?"

I said, "The good report is we are never going to be dog food. We serve a resurrection Lord. We serve the Living God. This is a picture of hell and what happens to people who worship the gods of the dead."

The Lord told me that it was a spiritual fortification that affected the entire world. The enemy was devouring the souls of three hundred bodies every day in this place while the families chanted and offered them to the Hindu gods.

There was a hostel on the island where the "eternal flame" to ignite the dead was located. The hostel was called the Death Hostel. It was where people waited to die and become one of the burnt sacrifices. We were not allowed to look inside, but outside the hostel, we watched families praying to the cows standing by the dead bodies. We watched dogs urinate on the dead that were lying there, waiting to be cremated. They took strips of cow dung and tied them to the bodies of the dead for luck.

I asked them, "What do you do with your god, the cow, when it dies?"

They said, "We grab the skin off of it and feed the meat to the dogs."

I told the man to give it some thought. We were amazed and grieved at the blinding of those that chose to worship the creation, instead of the Creator.

> For they exchanged the truth of God for a lie, and worshiped and served the creature rather than the Creator, who is blessed forever. Amen.
>
> Romans 1:25 (NASB)

The dead body was strapped with cow dung and then strapped to a stretcher. All the hair was shaved off the body. They offered the hair on the altar as another sacrifice. They baptized the body in the river called Mother God. The man in charge took fire from what they called the eternal flame to set the body on fire. They told us that the eternal flame had been burning for 3,500 years. When the body was burned up, they would remove the hip of the woman and the chest of the man. They held up these bones and chanted while offering them to the Hindu gods. I groaned in the Spirit as they offered the strength of the souls of dead people to Hindu gods.

The Lord spoke to us, "Seal off this gate of hell."

> I also say to you that you are Peter, and upon this rock I will build my church; and the gates of Hades will not overpower it.
>
> Matthew 16:18 (NASB)

You may wonder, how do you seal off a gate of hell? The Lord had us prophesy Matthew 16:18. We declared that Jesus Christ conquered death, his church would be built, and hell would not prevail. Then we thanked the Lord for sealing off the gate.

Hindu Temple Falls

We felt we had accomplished all God wanted us to do on that trip and returned to Jerusalem. Even though we did not hand out food, we felt we had cracked something open spiritually for Indian people.

About three days after we returned to Jerusalem, Mike was getting ready to leave at the end of a prophetic worship watch. I had asked him to remain for a few more minutes. I told Mike, "God has asked me to prophesy a judgment on a temple in India and on the monkeys they worship there." I said, "I know you love creation, but God wants to release his judgment. He is going to kill some of the monkeys that the people of India have been worshiping, and he will take a temple down. You and I can pray for mercy for the souls, that is all."

We prayed and asked the Lord to release his righteous judgment to kill the monkeys and bring down the temple. Mike said amen. Mike was so anointed and prophetic that he could enter the visions as the Lord released them.

A couple of days later, pastors from India contacted us and said, "We want to encourage you. Whatever you have been praying and prophesying, keep doing it. A Hindu temple just fell to the ground, and a hundred monkeys were killed inside." They also sent over a newspaper clip telling the story. No people had been hurt. I told Mike, "Now that was a successful mission trip!"

And the elders of the Jews were successful in building through the prophesying of Haggai the prophet and Zechariah the son of Iddo. And they finished building according to the command of the God of Israel and the decree of Cyrus, Darius, and Artaxerxes king of Persia.

Ezra 6:14 (NASB)

In my earlier years, I remember waking up one morning and seeing God standing at the foot of my bed. His finger had been pointing toward my mouth. He had said, "You speak it, and so it shall be." Now that we are planted on the walls of Jerusalem, prophesying the word of the Lord, I feel as if I am living in a wonderful and exciting dream. I want to encourage you to prophesy and watch while closed doors swing open.

Many people shall come and say, "Come, and let us go up to the mountain of the LORD, to the house of the God of Jacob; He will teach us his ways, and we shall walk in his paths." For out of Zion shall go forth the law, and the word of the Lord from Jerusalem.

Isaiah 2:3 (NKJV)

Isaac Rescued from Death

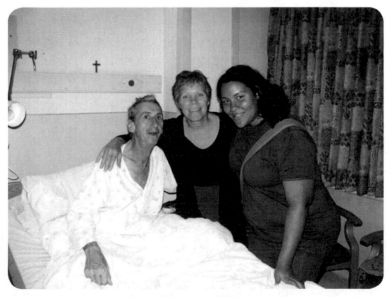

Isaac, Karen and Tamera

Isaac Nuseibeh

Isaac walked into church one day and said to me, "I have a lump in my throat, and I have to go to the hospital." Isaac insisted on going to the most religious Jewish hospital in Jerusalem. Isaac comes from a Muslim family but has been serving the Lord Jesus Christ since our early days in Jericho. Isaac's wife came to visit me and said, "The doctors said he is going to die." I thought, *After all we have been through together, how can Isaac die?* I knew God had a wonderful plan for Isaac and that his life on earth was not finished.

I immediately prayed and went to visit Isaac in the hospital. I told him, "God wants me to tell you that the doctors are lying to you. You are not going to die." We put a cross in his room and Christine, one of our volunteers, hung scriptures on his walls. We anointed his feet often and remained in constant prayer for him. I prophesied over Isaac, saying, "The Lord says you are going to live and not die. You are going to testify in the land of the living."

Isaac had surgery to remove his voice box, where there was a cancerous growth. After the surgery, Isaac refused to take any pain medication. Then when they did more tests, the doctors asked Isaac, "Isaac, what's going on? All the cancer is gone."

Isaac wrote on the white board, "Jesus."

The doctor said, "This Jesus you serve must be very powerful."

Later, the doctor said, "Even though there is no cancer, we want you to take radiation treatment." I told Isaac, "No way. You do not need any safety measure. Jesus said no. Do not take the treatment."

Isaac made the decision to go ahead and take the radiation treatment. The radiation burned half of his body, and he looked like he had been in a fire. He immediately stopped the treatment.

Not long after that, Mike had a dream that Isaac was going to supernaturally get his voice back. We told Isaac that no matter what the doctors had told him, he would get his voice back. Isaac had already undergone a tracheotomy. The doctors removed all his vocal chords, so he could no longer speak or even make a sound. Then one day, a few months after his release from the hospital, he walked in and wrote, "The doctors have said there is definitely a miracle happening. There is something in my throat now, and I will be able to speak again."

That day rapidly approached. Today, Isaac's vocal chords have miraculously returned, and he can speak again. He did not need a medical device; God did a beautiful, creative miracle. God is faithful and will come through every time for those who put their trust in him. Books could not be written to describe all the Lord had done for us in this very short time in the exceedingly good land of promise.

First Trip to Greece

Blake, Pastor Noubar, and Nehemias in Athens

One day, I walked out the door in Jerusalem to give a Bible to a taxi driver when I smashed my ribs against a metal rail. I was in such pain that I could not breathe. My ribs were burning, and I felt like my breath only went to the bottom of my throat. The next morning, I could barely sit down or stand up. As the week went by, the pain seemed to be getting worse.

The Lord said, "Go to the island of Kos in Greece and prophesy."

The pain was a constant throb, and I could not breathe. I felt like a rib was sticking into my lung, and I could not pick up my purse with the weight of my Bible in it. Years before, I had stopped using medicine, but I did pray about getting an x-ray. The Lord said, "It is not time for a doctor. Go now and prophesy in Greece."

We met with a church in Athens, marched in the Jesus parade, and were greeted very warmly by the brethren in Greece. The young men with me carried everything for me. It was a taste of heaven on earth, even though I was in great pain and cried as I climbed my way up to the Acropolis.

I was in Athens, standing and preaching in the same spot where the Apostle Paul had preached two thousand years before. It was wonderful. God had given me great favor. Visitors on the mountain gathered around me as I preached the same message from the book of Acts. It was awesome to know the cloud of witnesses was cheering me on.

From there, the Lord said, "Go to Kos."

When we got to Kos, I knew the Lord wanted us to bury scrolls and prophesy the fall of Babylon. We visited the first medical center of Hippocrates. As I was leaving, I bought a copy of the Hippocratic oath. They called Hippocrates the father of medicine. As I read the oath, the fear of God fell upon me. A part of the oath read like this:

> I swear by Apollo, the healer, Asclepius, Hygieia, and Panacea, and I take to witness all the gods, all the goddesses, to keep according to my ability and my judgment, the following Oath and agreement.

I was stunned. Almost every nation has used this oath, modified from the original Hippocratic oath, in one form or another. We began to understand how medicated and sickly the nations really were.

I traveled to visit the healing tree, an old tree in Kos. People come from around the world to visit this tree and believe the leaves are able to heal. They say that Hippocrates taught his students under that very tree. Presently, the tree is very diseased and shrinks in size every year. The Living God is causing a great famine in the streams of the counterfeit. One day, the snake on the pole will wither up. The Father will cause healing to come from the only tree of life and the one true source of divine healing—Jesus Christ.

> Then the LORD said to Moses, "Make a fiery serpent, and set it on a standard; and it shall come about, that everyone who is bitten, when he looks at it, he will live.
>
> Numbers 21:8 (NASB)

The Lord did not die to affirm the snake on the pole. He gave his life so that through Him, we would be delivered, healed, and given endless life. He is the author of a new and living way. When we are ill, our healing is not in what the snake did but in what he did on the cross at Calvary.

Upon returning to Jerusalem, I was completely healed as I reflected on the great work of the cross. He shares his glory with nothing and no one. Jesus Christ and he alone is all we need for this very great season that is coming to earth right in front of us. I realized I would never stand before the Father and tell him I needed anything but the blood of the lamb and the work of the cross. We will praise the King forever for what the Father has done for us.

> Surely he took up our pain and bore our suffering, yet we considered him punished by God, stricken by him, and afflicted. But he was pierced for our transgressions, he was

crushed for our iniquities: the punishment that brought us peace was upon him, and by his wounds we are healed.

Isaiah 53:4–5 (NIV)

For God so loved the world that he gave his only begotten Son, that whoever believes in him shall not perish, but have eternal life.

John 3:16 (NASB)

Justice Ministry

Living Bread International Church Jerusalem

Every Wednesday at Living Bread International Church in Jerusalem, we hold a service in Arabic. Pastor Noubar leads worship and preaches in Arabic.

One day, an Arab woman named Rodah came to visit us. She said, "The Jews do not want me. The Muslims do not want me. Can I become a Christian?"

I told her, "Sure, you can become a Christian!" We baptized her, and a few weeks later, she complained of being in a lot of pain. She said her leg was really bothering her, and she felt extremely oppressed. We knew in our spirit that demons were possessing her. She told us a Muslim man had died trying to do an exorcism for her.

We were in earnest prayer for Rodah, and in the name of Jesus Christ, we began casting demons out of her. She became restless, jerking her head backward and forward. As the Lord had us breaking curses off her, her eyes rolled back in her head. We prayed the blood of Jesus to wash over her soul, and the Lord told me to go take the cross off the wall of our church. While I held the cross over her, her fingers curled over unnaturally, and the demons in her began to screech. Rodah screamed and shook her head, trying to get the cross away from her.

The Lord gave me a word and said, "Nobody has ever loved her."

All of us prophesied and prayed that the love of God would saturate her. Moments later, something snapped inside of her. Rodah reached her hand out toward the cross and kissed it. She then took a Bible and held it close to her. The power of God's love and his great mercy delivered this woman from the demons that had held her captive for years.

Back when I had been living in Jericho, I received a visit from an Arab woman who told me that some priests in Jerusalem were abusing women, getting them pregnant, arranging abortions for them, and doing pornographic shoots with children. My friend in Jericho, who was a new Christian, asked me, "What do those stories mean? How are they connected with the church?"

I told him, "Those stories have nothing to do with Jesus Christ and his true church. The priests that practice those things do not really know him."

Weeping, I had a very hard time listening to what others were doing in the name of Jesus Christ, with crosses dangling from their necks.

Now, years later, in the spring of 2011, the same woman came to me again in Jerusalem. This time, she told me she was thinking of committing suicide. She asked me, "Will anyone ever help us, or will you sweep us under the rug?" Right then, the Spirit of God hit me. I telephoned my friend who worked at the mayor's office. I told him the story of the priest, and he said, "Be careful what you say about the holy icons because the pope himself has asked the government not to ruin his reputation." He also told me that there had been many legal cases against the priests over the years, but each time it was about to come out in the papers, everyone involved was bought off, and they never went to court.

We then started a justice ministry. We handed out five thousand flyers out in the streets of Jerusalem, letting everyone know we were offering free counseling for rape and abuse victims. Women came to our church and told us horror stories about abuse from priests and family members.

I felt the Lord telling me to go talk to the priests. The first priest I talked to threatened me, "People like you disappear. These women need to keep their mouths shut and respect the priesthood. Three hundred years ago, you lost your authority when you split from the Catholic Church."

I told him that when they walked through our door in Jerusalem, we had authority. The priest shocked me when he said, "Even if I am raping them, there's nothing you can do."

I told him to repent, or the judgment of God would surely come upon him. He grabbed me and shook me. Mike and Christine had to come over to get him off me.

Later, I went to see another priest that several people, including a tourist, had made complaints about. The moment I arrived, he asked me how much money I wanted. I answered him, "I am here for your soul." The fear of God fell upon him. Afterward, I told this man he needed to repent, or the judgment of God would surely come. God told me to pray for him. I mentioned this to the priest, and he told me to go ahead and pray for him.

As I was praying for this priest who had fallen from grace, I felt an undeniable, strong love from the Lord for his soul. No matter where you are, God is a redeemer, and it is never too late to come to the cross. Let Jesus Christ wash you with his blood and restore your life before it is gone. We are only here a short while, and the way we spend our days upon the earth will surely determine our eternity. The blood of Christ is enough to take away all your sins.

> Zion will be redeemed with justice and her repentant ones with righteousness.
>
> Isaiah 1:27 (NASB)

The Lord showed me a vision of a huge mountain of perversion over Jerusalem. I had a sword in my hand, and I was trying to drive it into the mountain. After that, David, a prophetic man who attends our congregation, came up to me and said, "The Lord wants you to walk barefoot in the streets of Jerusalem." David is a converted Muslim who has been burned, stabbed, beaten, and left for dead more than once, all for preaching the gospel. I admire him and feel he is a hero of the faith. Right after that, a woman named Lila Hunt walked into one of our meetings barefoot. I asked her how long she had been walking around without shoes on her feet. I was impressed when she answered, "A couple years." Of course, I obeyed according to the confirming word of the Lord. I walked barefoot during the night through the Old City of Jerusalem. One day, the Lord encouraged me with the following word:

> He makes priests walk barefoot and overthrows the secure ones.
>
> Job 12:19 (NASB)

A leader in very high authority from the Al-Aqsa Mosque in Jerusalem came to visit me. The man knew we were helping Arab women who had been abused. The sheik told me that the Arab people did not have a lot of understanding about social affairs, and he thanked me for the initiative we were running for the women and children. When he was ready to leave, I asked him if I could pray for him. The leader was in preparation to go to nations and rally support for the Palestinian bid for statehood.

As I prayed for the leader, the power of God hit him very heavily. He left without saying much, but the next day, he returned and asked me if I knew I had power in my hands to heal the sick.

I said, "Yes, I have seen many people healed."

The Temple Mount leader asked me, "Would you like me to teach you about the power?"

I told him, "Let me teach you, as I know the source of power and the God who gives it."

We agreed to meet again. I met him again later, and he asked if I would like to be on a platform with him and hold discussions about the differences between Christianity and Islam. Surely, greater works are in store for the city of the great King.

Patmos

Blake Davis in Patmos

For the last few years, people from around the world have prophesied to me that I should write a book. In the summer of 2011, I took a team to the seven churches in Turkey that are mentioned in the book of Revelation to do an antiterrorism workshop with our Gaza schoolteachers. It was a great success. At the end of the trip, I went with my son, Blake, to the island of Patmos, where the Apostle John received the revelation that became the book of Revelation, the last book of the Bible. My spirit was burning to go there. We went to the monastery and the cave that were the traditional sites where John lived and ministered. To my disappointment, I did not feel the connection in the Spirit as I visited those places.

At lunch, Blake said, "I thought you were going to take me to the beach."

I called to the waiter and asked, "Where is the beach?"

He pointed down the road, and we realized it was next to where we got off the ferry.

When we arrived at the beach, Blake went into the water. He looked at me and said, "Mom, I have never seen water like this before."

There was something unusual about it. I could not resist and went into the water with my clothes on. I felt the presence of God as tears ran down my cheeks. I told Blake, "This is an open portal right here. It is not the water, but the presence of God making this so awesome."

My heart exploded with joy as I came out of the water. I knew I had received what I had come for. I took a couple pictures of my son and remarked, "I cannot get the light out of the camera." Then I looked at my son and said, "I think John must have baptized people here. I know a move of God has happened in this open heaven."

When we returned to Jerusalem, I showed the picture of Blake to Mike, who is also a gifted photographer. Mike told me there was no way for me to have taken the picture with the camera. Mike said, "Never lose this picture, because there is no way a camera could have taken it."

It shows the touch of God and his light all over Blake.

Return to Patmos with Prophets

Karen Dunham in Patmos

While I was in Patmos, God had told me I was to return with a company of prophetic people. As I was praying, the Lord said, "Go early to Patmos and write this story." I was so excited as it was not very often I got to just spend days with God and reflect on all he has done in and through our lives. It was like being in heaven while I waited for the rest of the team to arrive.

We bought our tickets to Patmos. Then we heard from the Elijah List that God was dropping mantles out of heaven like that of Apostle John, the Revelator. That seemed like an extra sweetness. To be in Patmos under the portal and catch a mantle of revelation is for sure being in the right spot at the right time. Yes and amen, Lord.

A few weeks before the rest of our team arrived, I returned to Patmos with a scribe. In the hotel bar, they gave us a piano to use for worship every night, and the local Christians from Patmos would join us. One night, as I looked at the pictures on the wall, I became undone.

There, hanging on the walls, was a picture of Samson pushing the pillars. I thought to myself, "Wow, what a confirmation!" I identified strongly with Samson and the great glory he gave God at his exit. With one blow, God did a great thing for Samson. With one blow, I believed the portals of Patmos would open for his people.

A well-known evangelist was bringing a tour group to Patmos during the same time we planned to be there. When we arrived in Patmos, Pastor Larry, who was in charge of the tour, sent an e-mail that said, "We announced at dinner that you are going to be ministering to our tour group tomorrow."

We traveled with the tour group of 150 people to the theater outside the cave, where tradition says John wrote the book of Revelation. I was amazed that God would send buses of prophetic people to help with the weighty assignment. They were in tune with us in the Spirit, and we were very thankful.

I spoke about Samson and how he pushed the pillars with all his might and how, with one blow, the Lord gave him a mighty deliverance. We prophesied, "Push, push, push!" The presence of God led the way.

I went into visions and saw the wheel of the Lord spinning. It looked like a ship's wheel, and I thought, *Wow, God, you are spinning the wheel.* There was a shift taking place in the atmosphere as the Lord began turning things around. The Spirit of God was raining down on us. I saw countless white mantles falling from Heaven, and the mantle of revelation was coming through the portal just as God promised. We all began prophesying in unity, "Shift, shift, shift!" We rejoiced as the relay was released in the Spirit, and we all knew we caught a mantle and that we were a part of what God was releasing upon the earth. We were all in the right spot at the right time.

That night, we went to the ferry to say good-bye to Pastor Larry and the tour. A man on the tour named Nigel was in cold sweats and began crying out, "My stomach, my stomach!" He was lying on a bench in excruciating pain. We prayed for him, sang a song to God, and prophesied over him. The Lord spoke to my spirit and said, "Pray that the snake on the pole does not steal what Christ did on the cross." I prayed as he commanded. Nigel was still in a lot of pain, so we helped him onto the ferry.

A woman came over and said, "I am a doctor. You need to take this man to the hospital."

I told Nigel, "I saw the Lord healing you. You were in a black pool, and the light of Christ was on you. I saw the Lord pulling you out of the black pool. You are going to be fine."

As the ferry pulled away from the dock, the Lord said, "Keep on prophesying that the snake on the pole does not steal my glory."

The next morning, we got an e-mail from Pastor Larry. He told us they had airlifted a doctor onto the boat. By then, Nigel had passed out, and his blood pressure had gotten very high. When the doctor had walked over to see how he was, Nigel had suddenly jumped up and said, "Jesus healed me!" Then he jumped up and down while touching his stomach and said, "No pain, no pain!" Pastor Larry said that the doctor was also amazed at what happened.

The next day, we got another testimony from Pastor Larry, and he was so thankful he belonged to a healing ministry. A woman hit her head while she was walking to a cable car. As the day progressed, her speech became slurred. A doctor checked her and said that she needed to go to the hospital right away. When she arrived at the hospital, the doctors said that her brain was bleeding, and she needed to have surgery. Just as the doctor was preparing for surgery, he did another check and discovered that the bleeding had stopped. To the glory of God, the woman was healed.

God said to me, "There is a great shift coming to the earth. People will no longer rely on the snake on the pole and cures of men but will lean on my cross and be healed by my power." The Lord said he was going to bring a famine to the streams of the enemy. To be healed by his word and his blood is eternal and forever.

Those testimonies took place in Patmos as I sat in the portal of revelation with my new mantle and wrote these pages. As we walked outside of the hotel the next day, the shift in the atmosphere made the hairs on our arms stand up. We both exclaimed together, "The presence of the Lord has saturated the island!" We were so blessed as our friend Christine took us to the place at the end of the beach where I told Blake that John must have baptized people. There was a sign of John the Baptist there that I had not seen on my last visit, stating the very same fact. God is awesome, and he is a sovereign Lord.

 # The White Stone to Jerusalem

White Stone

The rest of our team arrived from Israel, and we chartered a boat for the next day. We spent the day prophesying in the waterways of Patmos. I swam to the shore from the boat, along with Richard, one of our team members, and we collected white stones. I knew in my spirit that the boundaries of the portal of revelation were being stretched as we picked up white stones and

God said, "Take the stones back to Jerusalem." God promised he would open a portal of revelation when we returned to the city of the great King.

It is so much fun to tarry in his presence while he fills you with power from on high. When we returned, we gave out white stones and prophesied, "It is time for a new name!" A lot of people have been given new names since we returned to Jerusalem, and even visitors off the street have said, "God just gave me a new name."

> He, who has an ear, let him hear what the Spirit says to the churches. To him who overcomes, to him I will give some of the hidden manna, and I will give him a white stone, and a new name written on the stone which no one knows but he who receives it.
>
> Revelation 2:17 (NASB)

One night, a week after we returned to Jerusalem, we were very high in worship and prophesied back to the Lord what he promised about opening portals of revelation in Jerusalem. Afterward, as we went outside, we were amazed to see a sign of an open portal above Jerusalem in the sky. Directly overhead, the full moon had a shining ring around it—a perfect circle surrounded by rainbow colors.

It was so large that it looked like it circled the entire city of the great King. As we began to worship and praise outdoors, an emerald ring appeared in another circle inside the cloud. God had promised open portals of revelation, and we were seeing the manifestation of the fruit of that glorious seed.

Apostle to Gaza

In Jerusalem, we were visited by an apostle who was being used by God in a mighty way with a church in Florida of fifteen thousand people. He was speaking to the leaders of Jerusalem and told them they have no power because they do not release the prophets and the apostles. The apostle said, "You try to build in a pastor's office without the authority God has ordained in the office of the prophet and apostle." As he spoke, fire came into my bones. I witnessed truth as it was being spoken.

Not long after that, a man named David came off the street and said, "God said you are his ambassadors." I felt his presence coming all over me, and the Lord said, "It is me inside of you. Look at what is inside of you, and you will know that there are no limits. Do not deny my name or the call I have given you." The Lord then said, "Go into Gaza as an apostle."

Another woman came into the church and said, "The Lord showed me a vision of you getting into an official car and gave me the word *rasoul*." I looked it up online. In Arabic, rasoul means apostle, prophet, and messenger.

I arrived in Gaza with my new mantle on my shoulders and went to the office of the Minister of Interior to pick up my visa. My file was missing, and he told our representative that the lawyer might have stolen it from the office.

I said, "How can this happen?"

The minister said to me, "Come back next week, and I will give you permanent residency."

As I walked out of the office, I felt extreme governmental favor had fallen upon us.

Even though it is located in a sensitive area in the Gaza Strip, I love showing Samson's neighborhood to others. It is awesome how Samson exited out of there in his death. God totally restored Samson, and with one blow, three thousand of his enemies fell. Oh, that God may use us to destroy the works of darkness that hold so many people captive.

As we pushed the pillars in Gaza, one of our friends said they saw light from heaven coming through my body and then flowing out into Gaza. In this spot where Samson exited, we picked up another relay baton. The Lord spoke and said, "Run the race to the finish with great power."

I said and continue to say, "Yes, Lord."

We will bless your name forever, God, for all you have done and are doing. The books written cannot contain your greatness or your loving kindness. Glorify thy footstool, oh Lord.

We say yes, we will gladly run with honor from where they left off.

We are singing, "We are taking off where they left off. Oh, on to greater works."

This testimony is about the power of the Holy Spirit through the name of Jesus Christ and our loving Father, who encouraged us and commanded strength for us every step of the way. To know this King and be known by him and to serve him throughout eternity is our destiny.

I pray to be able to push the pillars for the Lord just like Samson did, in the same power of how he did it. Samson may have started off rough, but he surely finished the race well.

Please pray about joining our team and serving the Living God in the city of the great King—Jerusalem. To visit us, tour the land, or help in the refugee camps, contact us at our office.

Living Bread International Church
info@livingbreadchurch.com
www.livingbreadchurch.com
Israel mailing address:
Living Bread International Church
PO Box 1056
Jerusalem 91006 Israel
US mailing address:
Living Bread International Church
PO Box 101 Cantonment Florida 32533 USA

Thank you for taking the time to read about what God is doing.